PENGUIN BOOKS

WHERE AM I NOW?

MARA WILSON grew up in Burbank, California. A beloved child actress, she's best known for her roles in *Mrs. Doubtfire*, *Miracle on 34th Street*, and *Matilda*. In 2000, she left show business to follow her passion for storytelling. A graduate of NYU, she writes plays, fiction, and nonfiction and regularly performs at storytelling and comedy shows. Her work has appeared in *Jezebel*, *The Toast*, *McSweeney's*, *The Daily Beast*, and Cracked.com. She lives in New York City.

D0956432

Penguin Books

where am i now?

true stories of girlhood and accidental fame

MARA WILSON

PENGUIN BOOKS

An imprint of Penguin Random House LLC
375 Hudson Street
New York, New York 10014
penguin.com

A portion of the essay "Writing Robin" appeared on the author's
website, marawilsonwritesstuff.com, as "Remembering Robin."

Photograph credits
Page 85: *Matilda*. © 1996 TriStar Pictures, Inc. All rights
reserved. Courtesy of TriStar Pictures.
115: Sandy Jensen Brandmeyer
201: Gabe Maxson
238: Avery McCarthy
228: *Mrs. Doubtfire*, Mara Wilson, Robin Williams, 1993, TM &
copyright © 20th Century Fox Film Corp. All rights reserved. By
permission of Everett Collection, Inc.
240: Monica Midbon

LIBRARY OF CONGRESS CATALOGING-IN-PUBLICATION DATA

Names: Wilson, Mara, author.
Title: Where am I now? : true stories of girlhood and accidental
    fame / Mara Wilson.
Description: New York : Penguin Books, 2016.
Identifiers: LCCN 2016019573| ISBN 9780143128229 (paperback) |
    ISBN 9780698407015 (ebook)
Subjects: LCSH: Wilson, Mara. | Actors—United States—Biography. |
    BISAC: BIOGRAPHY & AUTOBIOGRAPHY / Personal Memoirs.
Classification: LCC PN2287.W49225 A3 2016 |
    DDC 791.4302/8092 [B]—dc23

Printed in the United States of America
10   9   8   7   6   5   4   3   2

Set in Arno Pro
Designed by Katy Riegel

The names of some of the individuals depicted in this book have
been changed to protect their privacy.

For my mother, Suzie

contents

where am i now?

prologue

A FEW YEARS ago, I found a video of myself on YouTube. It's from what I like to call my "sordid past" as a child actor. Like many moments in my childhood, I have no memory of it, but I do have a record.

I'm sitting next to Robin Williams, who is dressed and made up like a woman. We're on the set of *Mrs. Doubtfire*. The director is filming us so he can see what Robin's makeup looks like on camera, but I don't seem to know that. I am taking it very seriously.

"What's your name?" Robin says, affecting a slight Scottish brogue.

I look puzzled. *"Do I say my real name?"* I whisper to the girl beside me, an older girl with long dark hair. (This is Lisa Jakub, who is playing my big sister in *Doubtfire*. She will go on to become my honorary big sister in real life.)

"It doesn't matter," she whispers back.

"My name is Mara," I say to him, quietly. It's obvious, watching it now, that I'm not sure if I was supposed to say that. He tells me it's a beautiful name and that I'm wearing a beautiful dress, and asks me what I like to do. I shrug.

"We could make up stories. Do you like to make up stories?" he asks, trying again. Five-year-old me sits up a little straighter. He has said the magic word.

"Yeah, sometimes I like to make up stories," I say. When I was a little girl, there was nothing better to me than a story. I loved books, and I liked telling my own stories, too. I don't know exactly when I started telling them, but once I did, I never stopped. Sometimes I would even sing them. And these weren't just anecdotes or neat little fairy tales—they were more like epic poems, tales of adventure and morality to rival Virgil and Homer—at least in terms of length, if not quality. A shorter story could take all day, and one of my longer sagas lasted the entire summer between preschool and kindergarten. It got to the point where, whenever I said "I have a story," one of my brothers would cut me off, applauding and saying, "Oh, good story, good story!" before I'd even started.

Unaware that I have yet to learn about pacing, and that this story could potentially go on for days, Robin asks if I want to tell him one, so I go ahead, launching into a story about a bunny who went out into the woods when he should have waited for his parents to go with him. It's a morality tale, full of suspense and a man (or rabbit) versus nature motif, especially after the bunny is thrown from his raft into a raging river.

Robin nods along for the first minute, but as the story continues, he seems to be wondering how much longer it will go on. Finally, I announce that the daddy bunny saved the baby bunny and lectured him, the mommy gave him medicine, and everyone had pie. The End. At that point, Robin lets out a low whistle, looks directly into the camera, and says, "We'll be right back."

I don't remember filming that video. I don't remember telling that story. Yet watching it as a twentysomething, I felt a remarkable sense of familiarity. If there's been a narrative theme in my life, it has been a need to find a narrative in everything. I found an audience as an actor, but even then, I spent all my time between shots sitting in my trailer, writing stories and screenplays. Adults would ask me if I wanted to continue being an actor when I grew up, and I would say, "Maybe, but I want to be a writer."

From the time I broke up with Hollywood (more on that later) and moved to New York City, I've devoted myself to stories, as a

Age ten, writing when I should have been watching my sister.

playwright, oral storyteller, and host of my own storytelling show. And now, here I am, once again telling my stories to anyone who will listen. Mostly, my stories are about being young and a little out of place. It's how I've felt most of my life: I was born the first girl after three boys, the only Jewish kid in my class, the only girl I knew whose mother had died, the only neurotic in Southern California (or so it seemed), and the only child on film sets full of adults. I was always in someone else's world, and I always knew it. This, I've learned, is a far more common feeling than I once imagined.

But not everything about my experience has been universal. A few months after I found the video of Robin and me, it was taken down, apparently due to copyright infringement. I had to laugh. Most people have embarrassing videos of themselves as children. Few have theirs copyrighted by Twentieth Century Fox.

the junior
anti-sex league

MY MOTHER COULD not have picked a worse time to teach me about sex.

One night, when I was five years old, she turned on the TV to a special about sex education. Kids my brother Danny's age were holding bags of flour, calling them their "babies," and scrambling to find "babysitters" for them.

"Why are they doing that?" I said.

"They're learning about babies, how to take care of them, and how they're made," she said.

"Oh." I knew the last part: they were made in their mothers' bellies. I had seen my mother pregnant with my sister. But now the kids on the screen were in a classroom, and a teacher was talking to them about cells and body parts.

"What's she talking about?" I said.

"She's explaining sex to them."

I had heard that word before. I knew it was a loaded term, something grown-ups only said in whispers. "What is that?"

"It's how you make a baby," she said, and went on to describe the most absurd, unappealing process I could imagine.

She had always believed in telling children the truth, at least to the extent that they were capable of understanding. She was open about private parts and calling them by their real names. Her instincts about openness and honesty were right on, but still, I was horrified.

"*You* did that?" I blurted out. She nodded, and with a sickening feeling I counted up myself, my brothers and sister, and realized she must have done it *at least* five times.

"Any other questions?"

I had only one more. "When you did it, did you say 'Whoa'?"

My mother had the best of intentions. She made it clear this was not something to be discussed in polite company, that it needed to be kept a secret. But I had a tendency to blurt out secrets. I have always been compulsively honest, and usually at the wrong times. Five months earlier I had ruined my father's birthday surprise party by asking, "You don't know about our cakes, right?"

Objectively speaking, sex seemed shockingly gross and ridiculous. But as the shock wore off, the world felt different. I could tell that sex was a Big Deal. It was something new and exciting, a secret grown-ups kept to themselves. Just knowing about it made me feel powerful. I had to tell someone.

And I had a big scene on the set of *Mrs. Doubtfire* the next day.

It was not my mother who had gotten me into acting. Not really. She was not a stage mother. But she was an actress: she had studied theater in college and never missed an opportunity to perform. My brothers and I went to Theodore Roosevelt Elementary School, and every year on Teddy Roosevelt's birthday, Teddy himself would come by, in person.

". . . And I said, 'Don't you dare shoot that bear!' They made a little stuffed bear and named it after me, and that's why we call them teddy bears today!"

"Teddy" was only about five foot two, with D-cup breasts and a hat I had seen in my mother's closet, but her performance was convincing enough to make some of the kids ask, "Is that really him? I thought he was dead." My mother disappeared into the role, morphing from a tiny woman into one of the most macho men who ever lived.

We lived in Burbank, in Southern California's San Fernando Valley, twenty minutes away from Hollywood. My mother always said of our hometown, "It's as if someone picked up a small city in the Midwest and plopped it down in the middle of Los Angeles." Burbank tried its hardest to stay quaint, but it was also home to Warner Brothers, NBC, and Disney Studios. The tentacles of the entertainment industry reached into everyone's lives. My father worked as an electronics engineer at CBS, NBC, and the local channel KTLA. Classmates came to school in cars with license plate frames reading PART OF THE MAGIC: WALT DISNEY COMPANY, and my brothers would borrow movie screeners from friends with well-connected parents when we didn't want to wait for video. Given the omnipresence of the entertainment industry, getting into acting wasn't an unusual thing for a Burbank kid to do. Children all over the world do ridiculous, borderline dangerous things, and no one around them questions it, because it's ingrained in their culture. So it was with child acting in Southern California.

When I was a toddler, the oldest and most outgoing of my siblings, Danny, started trying out for commercials. He was cute and a quick study, booking a few TV ads, and even some small parts in movies. Watching my mother and Danny rehearse, I had an epiphany. What they did was like when I performed my stories at home, only better, because people *wanted* to see you perform! Shortly after my fifth birthday, I went right up to my mother and told her, "Mommy, I want to do what Danny does."

"No, you don't," she said.

They were already starting to feel burned out. She was relieved that Danny had never become recognizably famous, and that he didn't want to be an actor when he grew up. He had been a confident, resilient kid, but the cycle of auditioning was getting to him. It would be worse with her anxious, oversensitive daughter.

"How about this," she said when I kept asking to audition. "Your brothers and I are going to pretend to be the people at a commercial, okay? We'll tell you what to do and then tell you if you got the part."

As always, I took playing pretend very seriously. I "acted" the lines about cereal or Barbies as well as I could, but every time my mother would say, "You were great, but you didn't get the part." And every time I would shrug.

"That's okay," I'd say. "I can just go on another one." For the first time in her life, my mother had no idea what to say.

I would follow Danny's example: get a few small roles, have fun with it, save some money for college, then give it up after a few years. I would never be famous. But after getting a few commercials, I was called in for a movie.

"So what would you think if your dad dressed up like a woman?" a man asked me, along with a few other girls who were

*Playing Polly Pockets on the set of one of my first commercials.
I was not happy with what they did to my hair.*

auditioning. The other girls looked at the ground, murmuring, "I guess it would be funny." I burst out laughing and said, "I would be on the floor!"

I got called back. And then got called back again, and again. We were called to do a screen test in San Francisco, and before I knew it, I had the part. I was going to be in a movie.

But just because I'd gotten the part didn't mean I knew what I was doing. There was definitely a learning curve. For example, how was I supposed to know what to do if I had to go to the bathroom during the pool scene? (My mother and I eventually came up with a code so I wouldn't end up peeing on the lovely and handsome Pierce Brosnan.) How was I supposed to know that asking some of the crew members to "clap for me" was inappropriate?

Everyone clapped for me when I sang in the kindergarten holiday concert. Why couldn't they do it here, too? My mother was, predictably, furious, pulling me aside and saying, "'Clap for me' is not acceptable!"

She and my father were determined not to let being in a movie go to my head. I always knew they loved me and they were proud, but they had to keep me grounded. If I said something like "I'm the greatest!" my mother would be right there to bring me back down to Earth.

"You're not the greatest," she said. "You're just an actor. You're just a kid."

The day after the sex talk, we were shooting a scene where we help Sally Field choose a dress to wear to her birthday party. Her ex-husband, Robin Williams, has been denied custody of their kids, and to spend more time with them, he answers her ad for a housekeeper and nanny. Robin, dressed in full drag as an eccentric Scottish nanny named Mrs. Doubtfire, was supposed to come in, ask about the party, and realize he had a major conflict. Lisa Jakub would say her line, then I would say mine. But I wasn't focusing on the scene. I was bubbling with excitement, because I knew this *thing*, this big open secret, and I could not keep it in any longer.

My mother had stressed that sex was something that happened only when you were married, so when Virginia, one of the hairdressers, came over to touch up my bangs, I impulsively asked her, "Are you married?"

"Yes," she said.

"Oh," I said. "So you've *done it*, right?"

She looked surprised, then laughed, embarrassed. She didn't answer, and I felt unsatisfied. As soon as she walked away I announced in a singsong voice, "I KNOW ABOUT SE-EX! I KNOW ABOUT SE-EX!"

The whole crew was laughing, and I was giddy. They knew that *I knew* what they knew! I was triumphant, full of pure childish glee—until I saw my mother standing off to the side of the set. She was enraged. When my mother was angry, she was terrifying. She looked like Margaret Hamilton as the witch in *The Wizard of Oz*, or Emma Goldman's mug shot. How many times had she lectured me about behaving properly on the set? How many times in our conversation had she stressed that this was *not* something to talk about in public? How had I forgotten both of these things?

I immediately stopped singing, and with a sinking feeling I knew I had done something bad, and that I was going to be in deep trouble. Instantly, I felt humiliated, and worst of all, I knew I had brought it all on myself. I thought I might start crying. I wanted to apologize, tell my mother I would never do it again, anything to get that scary look off her face and rescue what was left of my pride.

I watched as Robin, in full Doubtfire drag, walked up to Chris, the director.

"Did you hear that Mara was asking Virginia about sex?" Robin said, and they both burst out laughing. They both had kids. They had both worked with kids. They knew what kids were like.

"You know, Mara," Chris said, turning to me, "if you want, you can tell Sally her dress is sexy."

I didn't dare. But I looked to my mother, and her face had softened a little. I was still going to get a lecture, but because they

11

We always used to ask Chris Columbus when he'd discovered America. He would say, "Around 1976."

had been able to laugh it off, I had probably managed to avoid a spanking.

I stayed awake that night, thinking of how badly I'd embarrassed myself. It was the first of many nights like that in my life. Did anyone else remember? What did they think of me? I had learned my lesson, and too well. Sex was powerful, something I needed to respect.

But if it was so secret and special, though, why did it suddenly seem to be everywhere?

There's a saying that if a child doesn't learn about sex from her parents, she'll learn about it on the street. I learned a good amount about it on one particular street: *Melrose Place.*

"You have an audition for a soap opera," my mother told me

shortly after my sixth birthday, handing over my "sides," the script excerpt for the audition. "Your character's mother came from Russia, and her time here in America is almost up. She wants to stay here, though, so she gets married to a man named Matt, but he is actually gay."

"What does that mean?" I said.

"It means a man loves other men, not women. Or when women love women. It's just the way some people are."

"Oh, okay," I said. It seemed a little unusual, but not gross or disturbing. I thought of the girl at my preschool who had once told me she loved me and wanted to marry me. I had said, "Sure," so as not to hurt her feelings.

"Two men can't *do it* like men and women do it, could they?" I asked my mother a while later, as an afterthought.

"Not like men and women, no," she said carefully, after a moment. "It wouldn't work."

Lucky them, I thought, not having to do any of that gross sex stuff.

I got the part. My mother laughed when she saw the call sheet: next to my name it said "(K)," for kid: I was going to be the only one on set.

At first, we would tape my episodes and watch them later, my parents fast-forwarding through the racier scenes. But eventually my mother relented and just let me watch the episodes in their entirety. She had a strange barometer for what was appropriate: she was upset when I watched *Hocus Pocus* at a friend's house, but took me to see *Four Weddings and a Funeral* in the theater. To be fair, she must have figured I wouldn't understand what was happening on

Melrose—after all, I had thought the couple having sex in *Four Weddings* was just bouncing on a trampoline I couldn't see.

Melrose Place was the most terrifying show I had ever seen. People I knew and loved were playing characters who hurt one another in spectacularly detailed ways. Michael was driving drunk and doing it with three different women. Sydney was using drugs and doing it with three different men. Even Billy and Alison, the nice characters, were doing it, sometimes with each other, sometimes with other people. (Matt, my gay stepfather, didn't do anything bad, but that was because they weren't allowed to show two men kissing on TV.)

I had always wondered what grown-ups got up to when they weren't with their kids, and now I knew. To me, *Melrose Place* was

*With my mother and Doug Savant, who played Matt,
on the set of* Melrose Place.

an exposé on the secret lives of grown-ups. A little exaggerated at times, maybe—probably in real life there were fewer fights ending in pools—but at its core, I believed it told the truth, and I was scandalized.

"I thought you were only allowed to do it if you were married!" I told my mother.

"I said you *should* only do it if you're married," she said.

But they did it anyway. "Should" meant nothing to them. There was only one conclusion I could draw: children were clearly morally superior. Kids could be cruel, but it was simple and reflexive: you're in my way, so I'll push you; you said something I didn't like, so I'll call you stupid. But grown-up cruelty was premeditated, calculated, and clever. Kids, I believed, were virtuous because we didn't have that thing, that invisible, corrupting force that held all grown-ups in its sway: sex.

I wasn't sure if I trusted grown-ups anymore. I began to think they all had ulterior motives. When I started working on *Miracle on 34th Street* a few months later, there was a man on the set who bothered me: a warm, ebullient middle-aged man named Harry. He had a high voice, and he loved to joke with my mother. She would laugh and laugh, and I would worry, because I didn't see her like that with many people. Usually she was the funny one; the only person who really made her laugh was my father. Harry was in love with my mother, I decided, and I didn't trust him— especially not after the time I heard him tell my mother, "Darling, have I ever told you I *adore* you?" It never occurred to me that maybe Harry was not interested in my mother, or in women at all.

A lot of the grown-ups I knew in real life were nice. Most had kids themselves—so they'd *had* sex at one point, of course, but they weren't ruled by it. But others seemed obsessed with it.

When I was six, after I had just finished working on *Melrose Place*, I got sides for a creepy episode of *Picket Fences*, where a third-grade boy and girl hide in a closet to make out. The part was too old for me anyway, but there was so much detail, just reading it made me uncomfortable. It was obviously written by a sex-obsessed grown-up. They didn't kiss the way I had pecked my preschool boyfriend (which was only *after* we'd agreed to get married, and I still felt ashamed about it for years). They kissed deeply, like grown-ups in movies, and at one point the boy "started touching" the girl's chest. It felt wrong to me on several levels, and only seemed worse as I grew up.

People in Hollywood loved bringing kids into that grown-up world. They seemed to find it hilarious. Why else, when I was seven, would a journalist at the *French Kiss* premiere ask me if I knew what a French kiss was? Or the awful CBS News anchor who, on the red carpet at the premiere of *Nine Months*, asked me if I'd heard about Hugh Grant getting arrested.

"I, uh . . . Yes, I heard he was arrested." It was all over the news.

"So what's going on there, huh? What happened? What do you think?"

"I . . ." All I knew was that it had something to do with sex. Suddenly, I felt very small. I looked away, trying to see if I could find my mother. "I don't know."

At the Golden Globes that same year, I was interviewed for an entertainment show known for being a little risqué. The interviewer was a beautiful woman in a tight dress, with perfectly sculpted hair and eyebrows and an unplaceable accent.

"Zo, Mara," she said, "who do you sink iz ze sexiest man here tonight? John Travolta? Johnny Depp? Brad Pitt?" She raised her eyebrows suggestively at that last name. All I knew about Brad Pitt was that my mother thought he was overrated. Her celebrity crush was Anthony Hopkins.

I immediately felt annoyed. What kind of question was that? Who did this woman think I was? Leaning into the mic, I said, with uncharacteristic coolness, "I'm not like that."

Clearly, grown-ups didn't understand how kids thought about sex. To us, sex was gross or it was funny, nothing more. Sure, at every school there was always that one weird kid with his hands down his sweatpants, but surely he didn't understand the implications of what he was doing. Sex is nuanced, and nuance is beyond a kid's comprehension.

There were so many women at the Globes, all wearing so little. One wore a dress that draped loosely over her bust, and with only a glance, I could see her naked breasts.

"You know, Mom," I said as my mother drove us to Burger King after the show, "the men looked great, but the women need to go home and get dressed!"

She laughed uproariously. "You're absolutely right."

There was only one conclusion to draw: the world was corrupt. Everyone was corrupted. People were showing off their nearly naked bodies, having sex for money, doing it with people whose last names they didn't even know. "Casual sex," they called it—I couldn't even imagine being a "casual kisser." I knew someday I was going to have to have sex (if only because I wanted to have kids), but until then, I was not going to let it get to me. I would never be the flirty, dirty, sex-obsessed kind of grown-up. The only thing more powerful than sex was refusing to let sex have power over you. I was against sex.

* * *

"I think it should be against the law to *do it* with someone you're not married to," I told my mother.

"You can't do that," she said. "You can't control people's lives and bodies like that."

I would do what I could. If it meant being Roosevelt Elementary's one-person Junior Anti-Sex League, I would do it. When Mark MacGregor learned that "banana" could be a euphemism for "penis" and started chasing girls around the schoolyard saying, "I'm the Banana Man!" I went to the adult on yard duty and said, very sternly, "This is not acceptable." After one of the boys I sometimes played with at recess blurted out "You're sexy!" I went straight to my teacher and said, "Carlos said a bad word about me." I spent a lot of time feeling scandalized, and I loved it. There is nothing more fun than being young and judgmental.

"Do you guys know what strippers are?" I asked some of the younger kids who, like me, sat on the bench talking and reading instead of playing during recess. Sets were a good place to pick up all kinds of interesting information.

"No," they said.

"Oh, it's awful," I said. "It's so gross. It's . . . No, I shouldn't tell you."

"No, tell us, tell us!"

"They're women who take their clothes off and dance around while men watch."

They were so bad and wrong, and I couldn't stop thinking about them.

A group of kids would cluster around me every recess to hear about the scourge of nude magazines and exotic dancers. And these were the good kids, the ones who never got "benched" during recess, who got stickers and plus marks on all their papers and ran for class president.

They were as appalled as I was, and as titillated. Sometimes we would even pretend we were fighting the owners of strip clubs and dirty magazines, making the world safe again for kids. The bad guy in my games and stories usually wasn't a guy at all, but a girl who did it with boys.

"Once upon a time, there was a girl—and she was a really bad girl—"

"How bad?"

"Well, she wasn't a virgin," I said.

While I might never have admitted it, I was afraid of sex. It was a force greater than anything I could imagine. If anyone other than me was talking about it, I couldn't handle it. My cousin once initiated a conversation about penises ("Aren't they so weird?"), and when I got home I felt so guilty I locked myself in the bathroom and cried. My mother insisted I let her in and demanded to know what was wrong.

"I can't tell you," I said.

"You have to tell your parents everything," she said, so firmly that I wondered if it was an official law.

"Today I talked about stuff I shouldn't have. . . ."

"Is that it?" She was so relieved she almost laughed.

The first time I heard a dirty joke, I nearly went catatonic. I was nine years old and playing with the daughter of one of my grown-up costars. When she asked if I wanted to hear a dirty joke, I assumed she was going to tell me the same punch line Paul Reubens (better known as Pee-wee Herman) had told me when we worked on *Matilda*: "A white horse fell in a mud puddle." ("You wanna hear a clean joke?" said Rhea Perlman, standing nearby. "They hosed him off.") Instead, she told me one involving a little boy, his grown-up teacher, and the punch line "That's not my finger." I had a full-on panic attack.

It was hard to accept that sex wasn't just something bad people did, and it obviously wasn't something just men did, either. Every time I looked at a pregnant woman, I knew what she had been up to a few months earlier. Even my beloved nanny, Shoshanna, had done it. She had come to L.A. with the intention of being an actress, but hadn't had much success breaking into film and TV. The only show she landed was a sleazy dating show, and in a moment of grown-up inconsistency, she'd decided to use our VCR to tape it. She tried to mute it every time they asked something that was "too old" for us, but I heard enough. When the host asked, "So have you ever gotten down to business on a kitchen floor?" I ran out of the room crying. What she had done was against my religion, my own pieced-together theology. Premarital sex was a sin, and a big one, and big sins meant you wouldn't go to Heaven. What if the Christians were right and Hell really existed?

I worried for Shoshanna's soul until pop culture saved the day: I saw "Like a Virgin" on *Pop-Up Video* and learned that more than 90 percent of women had premarital sex. They couldn't *all* be kept out of Heaven. That just seemed like a waste of otherwise perfectly good souls. Still, sex was dirty, and corrupting, and I was going to be one of the 10 percent who stayed pure.

* * *

Grown-ups said girls matured faster than boys, but even when middle school came I never got taller than the boys, like they said I would, and the boys I knew fully embraced sex long before girls would.

"Did you know," my friend Nicole had told me back in elementary school, "that when a boy thinks about a girl he likes, his *thing* gets hard?"

"Why does it do that?" I had said. What did thinking about girls have to do with it? The mind-body connection was beyond me. To those who grow up without a penis, boners are magic. But what boys did with them—even if I had only a vague idea what that was—was disgusting.

Boys were so careless. Boys with their willies, willy-nilly, shooting semen wherever they pleased. It was why I always wiped the seat carefully every time I used a unisex bathroom: I didn't want the last customer accidentally getting me pregnant.

Boys hit a certain age and became natural perverts. I'd heard they thought about sex every seven seconds, and also every time they touched their belts or put their hands in their pockets. All boys looked at porn. Even my sweet, smart brothers had their stash under the bathroom sink—I'd stumbled on it more than once while looking for the toilet paper. (Nerds to the very end, most of their stash was not magazines, but erotic stories printed off the Internet.) When I met my costar Cody on the set of *Thomas and the Magic Railroad*, I thought he was cute until he said: "Man, the porno mags here in the U.K. are nuts. Not like

Playboy. Playboy's so boring. Here they show *everything.*" I was disgusted, but not surprised.

Boys were awful, and I was embarrassed that I was starting to like them.

The summer before middle school had been an enlightening one. In June, when one of my summer camp crushes, Jake, finally took off the baseball cap he had been wearing the whole week and revealed his messy hair, I looked at him and the word "sexy" came to mind. *Don't think that,* I had scolded myself, but it was too late. By August, my world had changed. President Clinton was under fire for having an affair with an intern, the number one hit in the country was "Too Close" by Next, about a guy who gets an erection when a hot girl dances too close to him, and I had slow-danced with two boys at camp.

"Something happens after you turn eleven," I wrote in my diary a month after my eleventh birthday. "You start to like boys. *Really* like boys." I was ready to be boy-crazy. Unfortunately, I had no idea how to flirt. Usually, I behaved the same immature way the boys did, teasing them, mocking them, being aggressive. I had blown my chances with Jake from camp after pouring Pepsi in his hair. I knew it wasn't the way girls were supposed to flirt, but I didn't know what else to do. Boys liked pretty, nice girls, and I was awkward and angry. The last time I had a boy interested in me—besides fans, who didn't know me as a person, and Jacob Hirsch in third grade, who was probably just happy not to be the only Jewish kid in class—had been the aforementioned peck in preschool. Having kissed a boy then didn't seem like such a big deal anymore, and it certainly wasn't shameful. At least I had been able to get some attention.

Back at school, some of the girls were catching up with the boys.

A girl named Christina made out with a boy in front of the school, and Jeanette was dating a sixteen-year-old. T.S.S., I called them. The Slut Squad. I hated them, and made sure everyone knew it.

"Mara," asked my brother Danny, "what do they *do*, exactly?"

"Well, they . . ." They hadn't really done anything to me. Someone told me Christina had made a face at me once when my back was turned, but that was it. They just offended me, the way they strutted around, talking to boys like it was the most natural thing in the world. I didn't want to admit it, but I was jealous. I wanted a boyfriend. I wanted someone's sweaty hand in mine. I wanted to know what it was like to be kissed. French-kissed.

At first I kept my urges secret. By eighth grade, though, something had changed. It seemed to happen to all of my friends simultaneously. Not only did we start to notice the physical changes, we embraced them: someone would make a dirty joke, and instead of feeling confused or disgusted, we felt *good*. It felt like a sugar high, but better. Hearts would race, palms would sweat, and bodies would tingle with an overwhelming feeling of anticipation. A wink from the right person, and I was on my own personal roller coaster.

That wasn't to say we actually had sex. For most of us, it was still abstract, even well into high school. For the most part, the people who did were "popular."

I had never been popular. I've heard that Dakota Fanning was homecoming queen and Blake Lively was senior class president, but fame never seemed to work in my favor. It could only be a substitute for good looks and coolness for so long. Kids I met at camp, on vacation, or at new schools would get excited and fawn over me for a day or two. ("So are you like a gazillionaire?" "Have you met Adam Sandler? He should write you into

23

the Hanukkah song!") Then they'd get to know me, realize I was kind of a nerd, and decide I wasn't worth their attention. It usually happened around the time they saw my roller backpack.

Aside from a small group of school friends—all girls, except for Alex, my former preschool boyfriend, who later turned out to be gay—the only kids who really understood me were other child actors. At seven I had done a photo shoot for *Disney Adventures* on "Hollywood Kids," and I had never felt so accepted. Everyone was like me, a little too smart for their age and a little too short, from sweet and pretty Lacey Chabert, to wry and witty Michael Fishman, to energetic and theatrical Adam Wylie, who would have been my make-out partner if I had taken that part in *Picket Fences*.

"You know what today was, Mom?" I said at the end of the day. "It was a pleasure." Except for when I accidentally elbowed Jonathan Taylor Thomas in the crotch.

If I ever got a boyfriend, I figured, he'd probably also be an actor. He probably wouldn't be, like, Disney star or *Malcolm in the Middle* famous, but at least he would understand my world.

So it was fitting that my first real kiss—or kisses, but I'll get to that later—came on a whitewater rafting trip I went on with a bunch of other child stars. Nearly all the child actors I knew did charity work. Some were naturally sensitive and sought it out themselves, some had gotten perspective on their privilege from traveling the world, and some had parents who pushed them into it to "ground" them. It was as much a social activity as it was an act of altruism. When I was finishing ninth grade, Patricia, who ran one of the charities, invited me and a couple of other kids on a weekend charity whitewater rafting trip. My parents wouldn't be there. I would be sharing a tent with Chelsea, a Burbank child actress whose sister had been on *Freaks and Geeks*, and a girl named Maxine, who didn't act, but liked charity work and loved hooking up with teen actors. My friends Tim, who had been in *Star Trek* and on *Malcolm in the Middle*, and Nicholas, who always seemed to play "that kid" in "that movie" everyone had heard of but had never seen, would be there. So would a slightly older and unbelievably cute teen actor named Greg, and four members of a boy band called Konniption.

When we arrived on a Friday afternoon, Patricia had the captains give us a tutorial on how to raft. I listened to them, absently rubbing sunscreen onto my legs. Tim and Nicholas sat nearby.

"Enjoying the view?" I heard Nicholas say. Tim laughed, embarrassed. I followed his eye line and my breath caught in my chest. He had been staring at my legs.

No one had ever looked at me like that before. Not in a way I enjoyed, anyway. Freshman boys would stare at my breasts, and an eleventh grader had looked me up and down while I was wearing my halter-neck show choir dress. Those times, it seemed to happen in slow motion, making me feel both attractive and vulnerable. But this time, it felt unequivocally good. I liked Tim, definitely as a friend and maybe as more than a friend, and I liked feeling his eyes on me. I wanted more.

It was going to be an interesting weekend.

After the raft lessons, we were supposed to spend time with the recipient kids, the ones we were supposed to be helping, the whole reason for the trip. We did hit it off with one of them, a boy named Darrell, who was our age, but most were much younger than us, and too shy. It was hard to relate.

"What are we supposed to do with them?" I asked Chelsea. She just shrugged. Her eyes were glued to Tim. We had already started to form a group, the three girls, the three boys, and Darrell.

"So which one do you like?" Chelsea whispered to me at breakfast the next morning. "I like Tim. Maxine likes Nicholas."

I thought both Tim and Greg were cute. Darrell was, too, with beautiful eyes, but he had a girlfriend, and even if he hadn't I wasn't sure about the ethics of flirting with a recipient kid. Greg was a little too cocky and a little too hot for his own good, but Chelsea had already staked her claim on Tim.

"Greg," I said.

It didn't matter. We all flirted with one another so much, I'm surprised we actually made it to the river at all.

"Should we tell them?" Chelsea asked when we got back to camp that afternoon, the three of us sitting around a picnic table.

"Tell them what?"

"That we like them." I looked to Maxine. She wasn't going to stop Chelsea, and neither, I realized, was I. At school I would have died if someone revealed a crush of mine, but here it didn't seem to matter.

"So guess what," Chelsea said when the boys came to join us. "We all have crushes on you."

"Maxine likes Nicholas," said Chelsea.

"Chelsea likes Tim," said Maxine. They both looked at me, and I shrugged, giving them the go-ahead.

"And Mara likes Greg," Chelsea added. Tim and Nicholas

seemed flattered. Greg seemed unimpressed, giving me a lazy thumbs-up and saying, "Cool."

I knew I should have chosen Tim.

Everything was out in the open now. We climbed into a tent together to talk and cuddle. My legs were on Tim's leg, my arm around Nicholas, my hand in Chelsea's.

"You know," said Tim, "if this were happening anywhere else, I'd be like, 'Oh my God, a *girl* is lying on me,' but here it just feels like it's not a big deal." We all murmured in agreement. There was something special about this place. The grass under the tent might have been grass sod, but we were away from our parents and free to give in to our natural inclinations. Hormones were rushing like the river. It felt so grown up.

"It's like we're adults," I said.

"Yeah, totally," said Chelsea. "Hey, did you know there's a ride at Chuck E. Cheese's that can give a girl an orgasm?"

A round of Truth or Dare was inevitable, and from there we went on to Kill/Marry/Screw.

But soon we got tired of hypotheticals. We sent someone out to look for a bottle.

I don't know why we thought we'd never get caught. It wasn't as if our tent—right in the middle of the campsite—was sound-proof, and we were loudly egging one another on the whole time, yelling "Kiss him!" "Kiss her!" while Greg blared "Hot in Herre" on repeat on a battery-powered radio he'd brought. The sun had set, and we were high on hormones. Poor Darrell sat watching while the rest of us started with cheek kisses, then mouths, and eventually started making out.

When we stumbled out of the tent for dinner, whispering and giggling, Patricia was standing there, her arms folded over her chest, waiting for us.

"We need to talk," she said, leading us off to a picnic table away from the main campsite. We were suddenly all very quiet. I had never seen Patricia angry. My heart was beating faster than it had all weekend, even faster than when I'd kissed Greg or pressed Tim to me and felt his heart against mine. This was a feeling I knew too well.

"Okay, guys," she said, in clipped tones, "I've been hearing a lot of 'Guess what the *stars* are doing right now!' It's one thing to do this on your own time, but doing it here makes us, as an organization, look bad, and you're making yourselves look bad. It's irresponsible and it's rude."

My eyes filled with tears.

"I'm sorry," I whispered, deeply ashamed.

"Are you going to tell our parents?" said Chelsea.

"It depends," she said. "If you guys straighten up and put some more effort into this—maybe wake up early to clean the campsite tomorrow—then we'll see."

Both Chelsea and I cried through dinner. We had known it wasn't right, but we had done it anyway. We woke up at six to scour the campsite and beg Patricia for forgiveness.

"You won't tell our parents, will you? Please? Mine will kill me."

She still didn't look happy, but she said, "I don't see any reason to." She had an organization to run, and bigger problems to address. I'd heard a rumor that Konniption had been smoking pot in their tent.

Chelsea and I were quiet as her parents drove us back to Burbank. On the ride home from Chelsea's house, my father told me, "You did a good thing this weekend, Mara," and I wanted to cry.

Once home, I shut myself in my room and flopped on the bed. All I had left was my guilt. It had all happened so fast. I would never even be able to remember who I had kissed first. Oh my God, I was a casual kisser. This wasn't how I was supposed to spend my weekend. This definitely wasn't how I was supposed to get my first kiss. Why had I done it?

But I knew why. Because it felt good. Because it was exciting. I had finally found something more fun than being judgmental.

I had always known my attitude toward sex would change, but I thought I'd always be able to control my impulses. I thought I could outsmart my instincts. If I were just bright enough and disciplined enough, I thought, I could outwit basic human biology. But I had felt it as much as everybody else there, if not more. In the end, every moralist is a hypocrite.

elementary existentialism

"Whatever became of the moment when one first knew about death? There must have been one. A moment. In childhood. When it first occurred to you that you don't go on forever. It must have been shattering, stamped into one's memory. And yet, I can't remember it."

—Rosencrantz and Guildenstern Are Dead
by Tom Stoppard, *the best fan fiction writer ever*

age seven

Some little girls plan their wedding. I plan my funeral.

Even before I have been to a funeral, I am sure I know what to expect. I had a role on *Melrose Place*, where someone died at least once a sweeps month, and I've seen the "November Rain" video.

"Bury me with lilacs, gardenias, and roses," I imagine myself whispering as I waste away. Maybe there will be a reporter standing by, like I saw in that one *New Yorker* cartoon, and he'll have those words immortalized in a magazine article about my life. "Or jasmine. Jasmine's nice. And freesia." I've also never smelled a freesia, but I've been to Bath & Body Works, and it smells the prettiest. I can't decide on the flowers, but I know for certain I want them to play all my favorite songs from different times in my life. This will become problematic in a few years, when my favorite song is the Divinyls' "I Touch Myself."

It's not that I want to die. I don't want to die. I'm not afraid I won't go to Heaven, I'm afraid I *will* go, and it will be like being in a dream. Not dreamlike in a good way, but in a surreal, blurry, every-thing-is-out-of-my-control way. Being asleep is the only time I experience anything other than my perception of reality, and I fig-ure that must be what death is like, except it lasts forever. I know I don't want that, but I *do* want a funeral. I always have.

age three

My great-grandmother dies, and the concept of death is explained to me. But while I understand what happened to her—my mother was forthright, as always—I don't think it will happen to me. In my mind, some people are unfortunate enough to die, but others sim-ply grow up and then back down again. I assume I am one of the lucky ones who will live for a good hundred years or so—"hundred" being the biggest number I know—then shrink and start over in the same body.

"That's what's going to happen to me, right?" I ask my mother and brothers.

"No," they say, "you're going to get old and die like Nana Becky." I immediately start to cry.

All I want is to live forever, and now I know I won't.

age five

My kindergarten class goes to an assembly on astronomy. The astronomer, in an attempt to make science more exciting, plays up the danger in the universe. When he talks about solar flares, I am convinced that come the next solar flare, fire will rain down from the sky and incinerate us all. By the time he moves on to all the ways the planet Venus could kill a human being, I am sobbing hysterically.

None of the other kids is crying, and I wonder if I'm the only one who understands. If this is what it is to be special, it's terrible. Several kindergarten aides take me aside to try to calm me down. When it doesn't work, they give me a rice cake and call my mother.

"Maybe you were scared because you were getting something out of it the other kids weren't," she tells me when she picks me up. "The other kids just thought, 'Oh, Venus, it's a planet,' but you were making connections they weren't. Maybe you really love astronomy!"

I don't think she's right.

age five and a half

My baby sister is born while I am in preproduction rehearsals for *Mrs. Doubtfire*, and my mother brings her up to San Francisco. She has told me that being a big sister is a big responsibility, and I have taken this to heart. One day, as my sister lies on the floor in our hotel room, I think it would be a good idea to tell her that everyone dies. I don't want her to have to go through the same shock that I did. She starts to shiver halfway through my lecture, and I immediately worry I've done something terrible.

"I think I scared the baby," I say when my mother comes in. "I . . . I told her about dying, and she was shivering."

She eyes me for a second. "She's probably just cold."

Later, I make sure to pick Anna up off the floor when the hotel maid is vacuuming so she does not get sucked up.

A picture I made when prompted to "draw my memories."
A few months earlier I had been kicked out of another kid's
art class for picking up a plastic model skull and doing an
"Alas, poor Yorick"–style monologue.

age six

My mother, perhaps testing her earlier theory that I am interested in astronomy, buys me a book on the solar system. And I *do* find it interesting, until I read that the sun will one day burn out. If the sun burns out, that means Earth goes with it, and so will I and everyone I know.

I panic.

Once again, everyone around me is unconcerned.

"Mara, by that time, we'll have space travel!" my mother says, exasperated. "Human beings won't even be on this planet anymore!"

I imagine millions of people fleeing the red giant sun as if it were a 1950s movie monster. They run screaming through the streets, hastily applying sunscreen, trying to squeeze into space-ships that are clearly not big enough for everyone.

"It's not like you're going to be around for it, either," she adds.

"I *know*!" I sob. "But what about my great-great-great-grandchildren?"

age eight

My Tooth Fairy, Sally (named after Sally Field), and I have a nice setup: I leave food out for her on my dollhouse table, and we write letters back and forth. My mother always helps me set out the grapes and chocolate chips Sally likes and reads the little books I've written for her. It's become a ritual for me, so I have to have it just right. But on some unconscious level, I know Sally can't come when my mother is busy or sick, or when there are people visiting.

I have two baby teeth removed while under anesthesia, but I'm too tired to remember to put them under my pillow that night, and my mom isn't there to remind me, because she's back in the hospital. The next day, all my aunts and uncles suddenly arrive from out of town, and while it's good to see them, I'm not sure why they're here. My mother has been sick with cancer, and she's been a bit worse lately, but it's been thirteen months since she was diagnosed. It feels like forever: to me, her cancer has become like my grandfather's diabetes, something she lives with and deals with, and probably will for some time. Besides, she promised me she'd beat it, that she wouldn't die. I put the little red plastic case the dentist gave me on the dresser in our front room and plan to keep it there until my aunts and uncles leave and my mother gets better.

My mother comes back from the hospital a day later. But she doesn't get better. My aunts and uncles are there to say good-bye.

A few days into sitting shiva, I walk into the front room and see the red plastic case still on the dresser. I think of Sally's letters, always written in my mother's handwriting, and my stomach sinks. My mother isn't ever coming back, and neither is Sally. There is no Tooth Fairy.

I leave the little red plastic case where it is. It will stay there for years.

age nine

Despite a Conservative Jewish upbringing, I seem to have missed out on the concept of Mashiach, the Messiah. While we're in the backseat of a van, a more pious peer—one of the few practicing Jews I know in the middle-class Christian bubble that is Burbank—takes time to explain it to me. She says the difference between us and the Christians is that they think Jesus was the Messiah and is coming back, while we believe the Messiah hasn't yet come at all. (The possibility of a female Messiah never occurs to either of us.)

"What will happen when the Messiah comes?" I ask, and she tells me—perhaps incorrectly—that the dead will come back to life, and we will all live not in Heaven but in a kind of paradise on Earth, forever.

"*Forever?*" I say, and my stomach clenches. "But what about the sun burning out?"

"God will take care of that," she says.

"But . . . I don't *want* to live forever!" I blurt out. Forever is too long, too big a concept for me. Besides, if everyone's coming back to life, does that mean evil people like Hitler, too? Or is he too bad to come back? And if he's too bad to come back, does that mean there's a point at which someone is doomed, maybe not to Hell but to some other place? Where is the line drawn? And what if there are people I don't *want* to see for all eternity? I always figured I could avoid people in Heaven, but Earth is finite. Or will we all get along then? And will there be animals? Will I be reunited with my dead pets? Wouldn't that lead to overpopulation?

In the midst of my reverie I hear her say, in her tattletale tone, "Mom-ee, Mara doesn't *want* Mashiach to come!"

"No! No, I do," I say, even though I'm sweating and shaking and trying to hold in my anxiety. "I . . . I'm just not ready for him yet."

age ten

I spend the day at a friend's day camp. At lunch, we talk about our families, and a girl asks me if my parents are still married.

"No, but . . ." I still haven't figured out how to explain without making people uncomfortable. "Um, my mom died."

"Divorce is worse than death," says one of the other girls. She's small and thin, with sad eyes.

"No, it isn't!" I say. An acquaintance whose father died several years after a divorce told me as much, so I knew for sure. "Death is way worse."

"But with divorce, you feel like you're being torn apart," says the sad-eyed girl.

"But at least they're still *alive*," I say. All the other girls around us have gone quiet.

"My mother and father are always fighting," she says. "My mother says she hates my father, my father says he hates my mother, he says he killed my grandmother by putting poison in her food, but then he says he didn't. . . ."

She sighs, as though her father's possible joke, possible serious murder confession is just another thing a child of divorce has to deal with, like not knowing which address to say is "home."

Now even I have gone quiet.

"Yeah, well, I guess they're both hard," I say finally.

age eleven

My nineteen-year-old brother, Danny, mentions that someone at school read his palm.

"They said I had a short life line, but a long love line." Everyone laughs.

"How is that possible? She'll keep you in the freezer?" a friend says, and everyone laughs again.

I'm not laughing. I'm superstitious, and to me a palm reading might as well be a death sentence. My beloved big brother is going to die, and die young. I cry that night and all the next day. When I try to distract myself by reading, I read *Bridge to Terabithia*, which only makes things worse.

age eleven and a half

Middle school brings out my morbid side. People routinely tell me I'm intimidating, or, in middle school parlance, "Oh my God, I thought you were *such* a bitch until I got to know you." I'm a four-foot-five cynic with a deep voice, an intense gaze, and a tendency to say things like, "You know what's gonna suck? When we *die*." My friends aren't sure what to say when I suddenly want to discuss the implications of an eternal afterlife—especially not the ones who are trying out for cheerleading.

Their enthusiasm for cheer makes me think I should try out, too, and, to my surprise, I make the squad. I'm not a good dancer or gymnast—I can't even do a cartwheel—so I can't help but wonder if I made it because the coaches thought I was depressed and hoped cheerleading would help. But I am dropped from the squad even before I get my uniform—not for my lack of coordination, but for amassing too many tardies.

I shift my focus to choir, where my contralto voice and flair for the melodramatic are valued, and back to my beloved improvisation classes, where I do what comedians have done for thousands of years: channel my misery into comedy.

age twelve

My father takes me, my little sister, and the woman who will become my stepmother on a day trip to Catalina Island. The sun is shining and Madonna's "Holiday" is playing on the radio, but I am deeply involved in my own thoughts. My concerns have been about religion, mostly, and what will happen if my religious beliefs—a mash-up of my father's Catholic guilt, my mother's own brand of observant Judaism, what I've learned from my almost exclusively Christian friends, and my own superstitions and obsessions—are wrong. I sit by myself on the sand, afraid to look at the sky: I feel like God is judging me.

All of a sudden, I think *Maybe there is no God*. I don't know what to do with this thought; it's something I've never seriously considered. *Okay, say there's no God*, I think, and a strange feeling comes over me. I feel lighter, but I also feel unsteady. It's thrilling, but it's terrifying. It scares me too much for me to hold on to it for more than a moment. I shake my head and go back to believing in God.

age thirteen

Every now and then, I realize I exist, and it's terrifying. It happens when I'm thinking deeply about my life, but it also happens when I'm just making faces at myself in the mirror. Suddenly I'm terrified of this Mara person, this identity I've constructed for myself, and it's all too much for me. My heart pounds in my chest and ears, and for a second I can feel a panic attack mounting, but then the moment passes, and I'm fine with myself again.

The next time I'm at my psychiatrist's office, I ask him about it before I leave.

"Do you ever have those moments where you 'realize yourself'?" I say, and immediately regret it. This is a topic for a longer conversation, something I should have brought up earlier in the session, before I started in on whether it was possible to be both agoraphobic *and* claustrophobic. He probably doesn't even know what I mean.

But he surprises me. "Yeah, sure, I have those."

"Is there anything I can do to make them go away?" I say. "Or make them better?"

He just smiles as he opens the door. "Learn to enjoy them."

I'm not sure how I'm supposed to do that.

age fifteen

I'm very absorbed in the *His Dark Materials* trilogy when the third book makes a good case for the nonexistence of God. It feels like a bait and switch: first I was absorbed within a beautiful fantasy world with just the right level of allegory, and then it all became startlingly literal. It's the same way I felt about the Narnia books, with their first-gentle-then-heavy dose of Christian evangelism. Unlike *Narnia*, though, *His Dark Materials* convinces me. It makes so much sense that I have to put the book down. It's all too scary, and I'm not ready for it. I don't *want* there not to be a God.

My stepmother, who is Catholic, sees me crying and says, "Maybe instead of reading the books you're reading, I could get you a Bible." I shake my head, but I don't stop crying, and I don't stop believing in God.

age sixteen

The term "existentialism" comes up in my arts boarding school theater history class. I scribble "Human beings are condemned to be free" on a Post-it note I will put up in the shower, where I put everything I need to remember for tests. It seems like an interesting view of the world, but then Chris Grabowski says it's his favorite artistic and philosophical movement and I can't like it anymore. It will one day seem absurd to reject a philosophy based on someone else's association with it, but I am young and Chris is *that* obnoxious. He once threw a fit when people were watching *Dirty Dancing* on the common room TV because he wanted to watch *Waking Life*, and he's always interrupting our theater history teacher with a smug "Well, *actually* . . ." Some friends suggest he's insecure, but I don't believe it: he's had leading roles in several productions and is dating a dance major, the art school equivalent of a cheerleader.

At some point I wonder if I don't like him because I'm jealous of him. "We don't like in other people what we don't like in ourselves," my therapist once told me. I've been the smart, deep one for so long, and now at art school *everyone's* like that. Chris is the deepest of the deep, and I hate him for it. But maybe I hate him because I want to be that pretentious, or because I secretly *am* that pretentious.

age seventeen

Jennifer, a moody creative writing major who was my friend until I found out she and another "friend" had both gotten drunk and kissed my boyfriend, comes back to school in the fall claiming she had an "existential crisis" that summer. *Big deal*, I think. *I've had those since I was five.*

I secretly *am* that pretentious.

age seventeen and a half

I am the star student in my comparative religions class. My teacher writes my college recommendations and says I have a "true talent for theological thinking." The world has pain and suffering because we are in the time of Kali, God is inside all of us and in everything, and one must kill the Buddha because there *is* no Buddha. Every week I have a different religion.

"I think there's a part of me that wants to shave my head and become a Buddhist nun," I tell my friends. "Or convert to Hinduism. I really like Vedanta." It makes me uncomfortable to think about it, though, and not only because I still feel tied to Judaism.

I keep talking about what I *want* to believe, or what I'd *like* to believe, not what I actually do believe. But what *do* I believe?

"Do you ever think . . ." I ask my teacher one day after class. "That . . . that maybe you just believe in all this because . . . you *want* to believe in it?"

"Those doubts are all in the mind," he tells me. "Remember, the mind can only understand what it can sense. There is so much out there beyond our senses."

He's so calm and certain in a way I know I'll never be. There is undoubtedly a lot beyond my senses—I'm learning this both in comparative religions and in the biology class I'm taking to cancel out the D in biology I got freshman year. The world is so endlessly complex, my biology teacher explains, that we need the scientific method to understand it objectively. He not only explains evolution, he makes sure we know how we know it happens, and that we can explain it back to him. There's something encouraging in this: the world fits together, and we can see how.

A few weeks later my one-person-show class (this is an art school, after all) takes a trip down to Los Angeles to see a one-woman show called *Letting Go of God*, by Julia Sweeney. It's a true story about losing her religion, and it draws me in. She has all the same questions I do, has the same encouraging feeling about science. But while I expect her to regain her faith at the end, she doesn't. Still, she seems like a good person, even a happy person. My parents grew up in the Cold War; they taught me people who don't believe in God are without any kind of conscience. But that doesn't seem to be true.

"If this is all there is," Julia Sweeney says, recalling a conversation with her Catholic mother, "everything means more, not less."

After the show, I walk outside into the sunshine, literally seeing the world in a new light. *Maybe this is how the world is*, I think.

Maybe God, the God I've believed in all of my life, does not exist. To my own surprise, I feel okay with this. I'm still afraid of dying, and the idea of oblivion isn't comforting, but I'm no more afraid than I have been in the past. Maybe deep down, I always knew.

age eighteen

I move to New York to attend NYU, and meet my first serious boyfriend, Sam, in a universally loathed expository writing course required for freshmen. He's a secular Jew like me, but he grew up in a wealthy liberal East Coast family, and his perspective is a little different from mine. When he shows me *Annie Hall*, I turn to him after young Alvy says there's no point in doing his homework because the universe is expanding, and say, "This is who I am! I *was* that kid!"

Sam eyes me for a second.

"Yeah," he says. "Woody Allen really has a way of making you see yourself in his characters."

He doesn't seem to get it: this proves there are other people out there who have the same kinds of fears I do. There are people like me! He grew up among anxious, self-loathing, leftist, atheist Jews, so he takes it for granted, but I am thrilled. I lived eighteen years in laid-back Southern California, feeling like the *Pet Sounds* to everyone else's *Surfin' Safari*. Even Idyllwild Arts Academy was sometimes too cheerful for me—after all, kids there called their teachers by their first names and played Hacky Sack for PE credit. But there is a place where people like me live and love while fretting constantly about their own mortality and the fate of the universe. I know who I am now: I am a New Yorker.

Maybe deep down, I always knew.

age twenty-two

Sam and I have broken up, and I have fallen madly, deeply in love . . . with science. My mother was right, I do love astronomy: the infinite nature of the universe both excites and terrifies me.

I meet Dr. Neil deGrasse Tyson at a book signing and ask him how he doesn't have an existential crisis every day; he knows exactly how insignificant he is, but he seems pretty happy.

"Your name's Mara?" he says, and I nod. "Mara, let me ask you something. Have you taken a philosophy class?"

"Yeah, I took ethics and logic and some other ones," I say. "How did you know?"

"Because only people who have taken philosophy classes use the word 'existential.'"

I am officially less down-to-earth than an astrophysicist.

age twenty-three

Some girls dream of dating a rock star. I dream of dating a scientist, one who will explain space-time to me and comfort me about my Higgs boson–related anxieties. A fling with a friend's brilliant mathematician brother grows into a relationship, but there are problems from the beginning. My putting him up on a pedestal, his job in Wisconsin, my obsession with death, his belief that humanity may one day be able to "cure" death.

"Doesn't everyone want to live forever?" he says.

I don't know what to say. The idea of living forever makes me uncomfortable, and at this point I've lived long enough and seen enough *Twilight Zone* episodes to know there's always a catch. The best situation I can imagine is dying, then somehow reemerging many years later, consciousness intact, to see what the future is like. I'd be the tiniest, friendliest Lovecraftian Elder God ever.

mid-twenties

Something strange is happening to me: I find myself becoming lighter and less cynical. People use sarcasm and I don't immediately pick up on it, because I don't use it anymore. When people do, it's as if I'm hearing a language I spoke fluently in my childhood, but have since lost. And I just find Woody Allen creepy.

My obsession with death has waned, too. I can now watch a YouTube video of puppies playing and not immediately think, *It's really sad those puppies will have to die someday.* I'm still not fond of the idea of dying, but it's not my sole preoccupation. Now that I have to worry about things like paying bills on time, feeding my cats, and where I put my Social Security card, I don't have time to worry about the heat death of the universe.

Back when I was twenty, one of my professors picked up on my grandiose anxieties. "When you're young," he said, "you spend time thinking about the world ending and catastrophes. But by the time you're my age, you'll just spend time thinking, 'I wonder what's new at Pottery Barn.'" My obsession with Pottery Barn hasn't kicked in yet (though I'm devoted to Bed Bath & Beyond), but now I think my professor was right—maybe existential anxieties are for the young.

Working with children seems to confirm this. At the after-school programs and camps where I work, I hear "God is dead" from both a wisecracking ten-year-old Manhattanite and a precocious seven-year-old from the South Bronx. When I ask a very intelligent six-year-old girl what she thinks about being the youngest in her family, she says, "It rocks! 'Cause I'll be the last to die!"

Somehow, I find it comforting. People may have to die, but morbidity will live forever.

the "c" word

WHEN I WAS seven, my family spent a week in Japan to promote the remake of *Miracle on 34th Street*. Within three days, I was ready to become an expatriate.

"This is *so* much better than the United States!" I told my mother as we walked back to the hotel with brand-new kimonos. Tokyo was electric, alive, and so much different from anyplace else I had been. An elegant, courteous woman in a kimono stood in the hotel hallway giving directions and advice in perfect English. The imperial gardens were a block away, full of pink cherry blossom trees and chrysanthemums bigger than my head. The Toshiba display screen on top of a building across from the hotel showed an animated light display all night long, like the world's biggest nightlight. And their Hello Kitty stores were *unreal*. It was a seven-year-old girl's paradise.

"It is beautiful," my mother agreed. "But Japan has its problems, too."

"Everyone's so *nice*, though!" I said. People in Tokyo were polite and followed such pleasant rituals: tea, removing one's shoes when going indoors, bowing to one another. Even the news anchors on TV bowed to the audience. It made me want to do it, too, and as we walked, I bowed my head to the people we passed. A Japanese businessman smiled at me and bowed back.

"See?" I said. "Everyone likes us."

They liked *me*, anyway. Our translator, Kuni, had told me as much. The entire Twentieth Century Fox Japan entourage loved my story about my tooth falling out in the cab on the way to the Sensoji Temple, and they all laughed when I put on a mock basso profundo to sing "When You Wish Upon a Star" at karaoke. No one even minded when I spit out a mouthful of shredded white radish I had mistaken for white rice! When *Miracle* was screened at Tokyo Stadium, I had gone out onto the field to introduce it. The audience wasn't as rowdy as the ones in New York, London, or Madrid, but we could hear them talking, and they were all saying the same thing.

"Do you hear what they're saying?" Kuni said after I walked off the field.

"What?"

"'*Kawaii*,'" she said, smiling. "'She's so cute!'"

It hadn't occurred to me that I was cute. My family told me I was beautiful, but I had never been one of the prettier girls in my class. The pretty girls—which I always said as if one word, "prettygirls"—were a different breed. They had names like Amanda and Marissa, which meant beautiful things like "love" or "the ocean," not "bitter" like mine did. They had been beautiful babies, born with full heads of shiny hair, instead of being bald for the first two years of their lives. They fit into the "slim" size jeans from Limited Too. They came to school on a Monday halfway through first grade saying, "I *finally* got my ears pierced!" It was probably as much of a shock to them as it was to me when I was cast in a movie, but at that time, casting directors were going for "the natural look," wanting kids who looked "normal." For the most part, this was true of the other child actors I knew: they were the most talkative kids in the class, but not necessarily the most beautiful. As long as we could memorize our lines and say them with some feeling, no one cared how symmetrical our faces were. And it had worked: I had tricked entire countries into thinking I was cute.

When I was cast in the remake of *Miracle on 34th Street*, Twentieth Century Fox had just had a major hit with *Home Alone* and was trying to find a way to further capitalize on America's apparent love of Christmas movies and mischievous young boys. John Hughes had been assigned to write the script, and the part of Susan, the young girl played by Natalie Wood in the original, had been rewritten as a boy named Jonathan. Christopher Columbus, who directed both *Home Alone* and *Mrs. Doubtfire*, must have put in a good word for me, because the sides for Jonathan ended up in my mother's hands.

"What's it about?" I asked, never having seen the original.

"It's about a little girl who doesn't believe in Santa Claus," she said.

"Oh," I said. "Is she Jewish like us?"

She told me she'd look into it, and gave me the sides. I liked Jonathan/Susan right away; she seemed smart. Where Natalie in *Doubtfire* and Nikki on *Melrose Place* hadn't seemed like real people, just accumulations of reactions to the other characters, Susan felt like a real kid, someone with wants and needs. A few days later I read my lines for the production team and told them I didn't believe in Santa Claus, but I did believe in the Tooth Fairy and had named mine after Sally Field. They laughed, thanked me for my audition, and within a few weeks had changed Jonathan back to Susan. I had the part.

With Jack McGee, who played the bad Santa.

Both my mother and I liked John Hughes right away. He didn't talk down to me, and he was from the same suburb of Chicago that she was. But I could sense my mother's doubts about the remake. While we both trusted John, he didn't have much say anymore: once a film is in production, the script no longer belongs to the screenwriter. Every day on set is a communal editing and rewriting process, and major changes are often done at the behest of the director, producers, or stars. And so it went on *Miracle*. John Hughes was still reeling from the death of his close friend John Candy, and took an even more laissez-faire approach than usual. Script changes were mostly left to our director.

The director was young, without much professional experience, and I never knew how I felt about him. He always seemed to make what we were doing in a scene into a joke.

"So Sir Richard is going to look up at you through the window and wave, and you're going to yank the curtain across really fast, like someone walked in on you in the shower! Like, 'Don't come in, I'm naked!'" I giggled, but when I looked to my mother, she wasn't smiling. Her instinct was to keep it professional and not interfere, but it had always been hard for her to keep her opinions to herself.

"Are you sure you want Mara to say 'uncharacteristically'?" she asked him after a rewrite. "She's still getting over her lisp."

Of course he wanted me to. Didn't she get it? It was *adorable* to make a six-year-old with a speech impediment say an eight-syllable word. My mother was annoyed, and I could tell. As the months went on, she went from furtively asking "Are you sure?" to demanding to know why a change was being made.

"Why is she saying 'crap'?"

"Why is she rolling her eyes at her mother?"

"Why is she wearing a hair ribbon to *bed*?"

"Well, you know," he would say. "It's cute."

I could sense her disappointment. They were making Susan as cute as possible, and taking away what had drawn us to her— her intelligence and complexity. She was becoming a caricature.

My mother didn't care for cuteness. She had never been one

of the "prettygirls," either; she was the living embodiment of the trope where a woman is said to be "not beautiful," but so "charming" and "vivacious" people cannot help but find her attractive. "Your mother is a wonderful woman," someone—a PTA member, a producer, Dylan McDermott—would tell me at least once a week, and I'd glow with pride on her behalf. But I was starting to notice how, whenever we were around someone particularly beautiful, my mother would stiffen and stand up a little straighter. If they were pleasant to be around, she would acknowledge their good looks, but if they weren't, she'd immediately write them off as an "idiot."

All through the last few months of *Miracle* and our publicity tour, she smiled whenever people told her I was cute, but I could sense she was forcing it. Her disapproval was contagious: it never occurred to me that I didn't have to share her opinions. Japan was the last place I felt comfortable being called "cute." After that, anytime someone said it, I would wince. Something about it made me feel smaller.

We came back to a house cluttered with *Miracle* tote bags, posters bigger than I was, and sweatshirts with *Milagro en la Ciudad* plastered across the chest. There was also a large box addressed to me, which my mother opened.

"What is it?" I asked her.

"It's Shirley Temple movies, from Fox," she said. "They're saying they want you to be the next Shirley Temple."

"Oh."

My mother's expression was neutral, but I could already tell this was something she didn't want. I wasn't sure it was what I wanted, either. We watched *Bright Eyes* and *The Little Princess* and I thought about how I'd say no to this. Shirley Temple was so cute, she didn't quite seem real. Did I admire her? Yes. Did I want to *be* her? No. My mother knew, and I was starting to sense, that being cute meant being controlled, and that being the next Shirley Temple would mean everyone in the world knowing a version of Mara Wilson that wasn't me at all.

The film version of me was already polarizing. Some outlets loved me: *Entertainment Tonight* asked me back again and again, and gave me a special segment when I lost a tooth in the middle of an interview. Others weren't feeling it. One woman at a film magazine I'll call *Entertainment Twice-a-Fortnight* was particularly brutal, referring to me as "Mara Wilson, who lisped her way over-fetchingly through *Mrs. Doubtfire* and continues the tiresome act here." She devoted an article to "the risks of being too cute as a child actor," but rather than complain about directors and producers who treated children like dolls, she reserved her ire for me. When she saw me smile, all she wanted was—and these are her own words—"to shake her by her tiny adorable shoulders until her little Chiclet teeth rattle."

In some ways, it couldn't be helped. The writer had been writing film reviews for them for only a few months, and it was still the early nineties. Grunge and nihilism were in. What better way to show one's edgy coolness than hypothetical child abuse?

A few months later the same magazine asked me to appear in their issue dedicated to *Melrose Place*, then referred to me as "nauseatingly sweet."

"Well, they have a point," my mother said. "Some of the stuff they had you doing was a little . . ." She put her hands to her cheeks and batted her eyelashes. "You know. It was cutesy." But it wasn't as if I'd asked for that. I didn't want to be cute. I wanted to be *me*.

"Can't I play someone tough sometime?" I asked her, once we were finally done promoting *Miracle*. "Like a tomboy, or even someone kind of bratty?"

But we both knew people didn't really write those parts for young girls. Adults couldn't even get little boys right: no preteen boy still called his father "Daddy," and no kid ever said, "I'm only a kid," unless they were trying to get out of trouble. Their girl characters were even more unbelievable: the few times they weren't "nauseatingly cute," they made too many fart or sex jokes. They weren't real tough or bratty girls; they were Kevin McCallister from *Home Alone*, with longer hair.

"If they like you enough," my mother said, "they may change a part for you." It had happened on *Miracle*—at least in the beginning—and since being cast as the title character in *Matilda* six months before, I had some clout. When a script came in for a character described as "girly," she dressed me for the audition in some of my brothers' hand-me-downs.

"I want them to see there's more to you than being cute," she said. I did not get the part.

Puberty is a completely natural phenomenon. So are earthquakes and hurricanes.

"Whatever happened to Anthony Michael Hall?" I once asked Jamie, one of the caretakers who watched me on various sets when I was a bit older. "He was so cute in *Sixteen Candles*."

"He's still in stuff," she said. "But . . ."

"But what?"

"But . . ." She hesitated. "Sometimes . . . really cute child actors don't always grow up to be the cutest grown-ups."

"Oh, I know that," I said, almost too dismissively. I was only a preteen, but I was wise to the world. That may have happened to them, but it wouldn't happen to me. It only seemed to happen to the ones who did drugs, and I had been a spokesperson for D.A.R.E.

Head shot, age eleven. So cool, so edgy,
so should have taken off the Tigger watch.

Then I wondered: did they do drugs because they weren't cute any-more and were sad, or did the drugs come first? Either way, it didn't matter, because I was going to be pretty when I grew up. I knew this because once my brother Danny had seen a young woman who "looked like Mara fifteen years from now" and had said she was "really pretty."

I couldn't wait to get older. When Kiami Davael, who played Matilda's best friend, Lavender, had turned nine while we were filming, she had been allowed to work for another hour a day. It had seemed like a rite of passage; I couldn't *wait* to work nine hours a day. But that wasn't all: I wanted the freedom my teenage brothers had, wanted to do all the cool things they did, like driv-ing and going to concerts without a chaperone. From the time I was eight, the year I'd shot *Matilda* and lost my mother to can-cer, my father had become so overprotective, he wouldn't even let me cross the street by myself. Most of all, though, I wanted people to stop thinking I was younger than I was.

There was a power I had on film sets, something that, as a mid-dle child and a public school student, I'd never had before. Even if the role itself was "nauseatingly sweet," people on the set took me seriously because they *had* to; I was helping to make the movie happen. This power did not translate into real life. People in real life don't take children very seriously, especially if they're short and "cute." So when someone said, "You're so cute," I heard, "You're so *young*." I was young, and I didn't matter.

Even the most innocuous comments seemed insulting. When a friendly woman in a shop told me, "My granddaughter is about your age. I bet you're about seven or eight, aren't you?" I responded, "I'm *nine*." There was a big difference.

For a few years after that, I ended up passing on most of the scripts that came my way. The characters were too young— anything where my character called her parent "Mommy" or "Daddy" was out. When I came home one day in sixth grade and opened up one of those familiar heavy manila envelopes, I had a visceral reaction to the script's title. *Thomas and the Magic Railroad*? Ugh. How *cute*. I'd already turned down *Barney's Great Adventure*; did they really think I was going to say yes to this?

"You do have to say yes to some projects if you want to keep acting," my father said, but I shook my head. I did want to keep working, but on my own terms.

"Look," he said, a little exasperated, "if you do it, it'll be a short shoot, it'll be out in the British Isles, it will be fun. We're going to meet with the director, okay? She's supposed to be really nice."

She *was* really nice. Britt Allcroft was a gentle, slightly eccentric, grandmotherly woman who was full of ideas, and I couldn't say no to her. I took the part when it was offered. The kids at school might make fun of me for being in a little kids' movie, but, like my dad said, it would be fun. I'd get to travel to the beautiful Isle of Man, work with Frenchy from *Grease* and two very cute male costars, and I would get paid. I hadn't thought much about the money I was making when I was younger—my parents had always put it aside for my education—but I was eleven and college wasn't too far away.

We filmed for a month on the Isle of Man, and I went back to school to start seventh grade. The day after Halloween, I had to fly out to Toronto for a month to do interior scenes on a soundstage. My father had to work so I went on my own. I arrived sleep-deprived and with a sugar hangover, and I didn't notice the worried glances among the production team.

A week into filming, my stylish Londoner caretaker on set, Lucy, told me Britt was coming into the trailer to talk to me.

"About what?"

"She just needs to have a private conversation with you."

Private? I couldn't imagine what this was going to be about.

Lucy went into the tiny bedroom at the back of the trailer and shut the door. A moment later Britt ascended the stairs and sat down next to me on the couch, looking serious.

"Mara, when we first started filming, you were eleven, still a little girl, but now you're a grown-up twelve-year-old...."

I had an uneasy feeling, the same kind that comes from knowing an adult is about to talk to you about sex and there is no way to stop it from happening.

"... And there's a difference, a difference in your body. We've noticed it when we watch the dailies. So, maybe if you could wear a sports bra ..."

It wasn't as if I hadn't been wearing one. I had since fifth grade, when my nanny Shoshanna had looked at me in a tight, stretchy shirt and announced, "We need to get you a bra."

She'd taken me shopping the next week, and I was surprised to find I was nervous. My friends and I had giggled and gossiped about when we would need bras and get our periods, but now that it was more than a hypothetical, it wasn't exciting anymore. It was just scary. When I looked at my bra-clad self in the department store mirror, I didn't feel like I was growing up, but like I was growing further away from myself.

Britt got up to leave. I closed the door behind her and walked to the bedroom, feeling numb. Lucy was laying out some white sports bras on the bed. They looked like they were made of rubber, meant more for binding my chest than for supporting it.

"Louis gave me some new bras for you," she said. My gaze met hers, and I knew she had noticed, too. They had all discussed this beforehand without my knowledge. Puberty had arrived, and I was the last to know.

"I know it's embarrassing, but you really can tell the difference," she said gently.

I nodded and looked down at the floor again, tears stinging my eyes. Why did I feel like I had done something wrong?

"Oh, don't look so sad," Lucy said, giving my shoulder a squeeze. "It's not a bad thing. Boobs are *fab!*"

By the time we finished filming and I went back to school, my training bras were so small the cups were more like pasties. Getting my period a few months later was scary and startling, but not that much of a surprise; I'd seen that Always-sponsored video in fourth and fifth grade and knew that aspect of puberty usually followed the other. I had never felt so alienated from my own body. It would have been uncomfortable enough in private, but I was going through it under public scrutiny.

One day I made the mistake of looking myself up on the Internet. A website called Mr. Cranky wrote that I was popping up in every movie these days because I would soon be entering "the awkward years, when she'll be old enough to have breasts, but not old enough to show them legally." I folded my arms over my chest just reading that, and even as an adult it makes me shudder. Who did they think they were, talking about a preteen girl's breasts?

It got worse, much worse. The next page of search results linked to a website with a description that said, "If you want Mara Wilson nude and sex pictures, click here."

My stomach dropped and my heart pounded as I desperately tried to make sense of it. Maybe there was some kind of porn actress who had the same name as me. Or what if . . . what if I had been drugged and kidnapped and raped and then somehow made to forget the whole thing? I took a gulp of air and some rational part of my brain remembered that there was such a thing as photo manipulation, that they could take a picture of my head and put it on someone else's body. But that didn't make me feel any better: who was this poor anonymous girl whose body stood in for mine? I burst into tears.

All day long, I cried. I didn't want to tell my father. It wasn't my fault, I knew, but I still felt ashamed. My father wouldn't let me go to bed without telling him why I was crying, but I had no words to describe it.

"I . . . looked myself up on the Internet and I was . . . upset by what I saw," I told him eventually. I couldn't look at him. "People are using my pictures and . . . I don't know, making things with it."

"You mean, like pornography?"

"I . . . think so." I sniffled.

He was quiet for a long time, but ultimately reassured me. This happened to a lot of actresses, sadly, he told me. We were fortunate to have lawyers who could go after the people who were spreading this, and it was going to be okay.

It was just the beginning. A few months later I found out I was listed on a foot fetish site that cataloged scenes in movies where children's feet could be seen. Then there was the fan letter from an adult man who said he loved my legs and wanted my lip print on an index card. There was even a rumor on IMDb that I had died of a broken neck in Bridgeport, Connecticut.

I tried to laugh it off, but the laughs always felt hollow. Being a celebrity meant being vulnerable. It meant my face, my body, even my death were for public consumption—none of them was mine alone.

Still, it wasn't as if I was going to stop acting. I didn't know how, and I didn't want to. But I wasn't a little kid anymore, and it was getting more difficult to pretend to be one. *Thomas* was going to be my last film as a little girl, and, I decided, my last kids' movie. It was time for grown-up movies.

My father clearly did not agree. Anytime anyone asked him about my acting, he made sure to let them know that "Mara's mother and I always thought there weren't enough good kids'

On the phone with Lucy on my thirteenth birthday,
which was spent in a Toronto hotel promoting Thomas.

movies out there," and that that was why I did so many of them. We might have given up on the "good" part a few years earlier, but kids' movies were what we did.

"Can't I try out for parts in some more grown-up movies?" I asked him. "Please?"

He looked worried. But he always looked worried. Ever since I started puberty, I got the feeling my father was afraid to interact with me—maybe because, as he would freely admit, he had never been able to understand women, and I was a "woman" now. He had always left the "girl stuff" to my mother. In fact, he'd left most of the difficult parts of child rearing to my mother, preferring to be the Good Cop. Now he had to deal with his already sensitive, temperamental daughter's adolescent angst and awkwardness, and I could tell he was overwhelmed. It was why I never told him I got my period.

"I don't know," he said. "Let's just see what comes along. We don't want to pick one that's too old for you."

What did he mean, "too old"? I thought. I was almost thirteen.

We got a few grown-up movie scripts: a miniseries remake of *The Exorcist*, an adaptation of *Divine Secrets of the Ya-Ya Sisterhood* that I liked more than I wanted to admit, and Oscar bait about childhood cancer and near-death experiences called *Dragonfly*. By far, the most interesting of them was an independent film called *The Safety of Objects*.

I opened the manila envelope when my father wasn't home and the script fell open to a page with two teenage girls *smoking*. My character *smoked*! Only bad girls smoked! I was elated. I flipped around some more. There was talk of a preteen boy having sex with a Barbie doll. Sex, drugs, affairs, masturbation, kidnapping, violence, death, betrayal—everything salacious and miserable, all the apparent horrors lurking below the benign banalities of the sub-urbs, they were all in this script. As in every late-nineties independent movie, the characters' plotlines all connected at the end, and, as in most, it didn't quite make sense. I wasn't sure what the *story* was, but it was too juicy to pass up.

"Dad," I said as soon as he came home, "I want to audition for this one."

The next day I took the script to school. My friends and I usually read the dirtier parts of one of Alex's Stephen King books out loud at lunch, but that day we just passed around the script.

"Guys! Guys! Listen to this," said Alex, and put on a mock-girly voice. "'It's soft! I thought it would be hard, like wood!'"

"Is that the part you're reading for, Mara?" asked my friend Melissa, amid the squeals of laughter.

"No, I'm supposed to be reading for this other character. She's, like, totally androgynous. You're not supposed to know for sure if she's a boy or a girl until the end of the movie."

"They want *you* to play a boy?" said Alex. A few months earlier he had started calling me "Carmen Electra" after I had attempted to jog across our school's front lawn in a very unsupportive bra.

"Yeah, I don't know if you could do that," said Sierra.

"Sure she could," Melissa said. "She'd just have to tape them down."

"She's a C-cup," said Sierra. "It's not gonna happen." She and I wore the same bra size, true bosom buddies. When we wanted to hug each other, we had to bend at a nearly ninety-degree angle.

"Wear a sports bra," suggested Charlotte. "Wear two."

"We could ask people what they think," I said, half joking.

Melissa rolled her eyes. "You just want people to talk about your boobs."

"Well, yeah," Alex said to her. "Wouldn't you, if you had boobs like hers?" Melissa hit him in the arm.

After lunch, I polled all the male members of my U.S. history class. "Do you think I could play a boy?" One after another, they all gave me the same response: a quick glance downward and a definitive "No." I didn't want to admit it, but Melissa was right: it felt good. No one had called me cute or mentioned the way I looked in years, at least not in a positive way. My sixth-grade crush had called me ugly, film reviewers said I was "odd-looking," and a boy at my preteen day camp had said to me, "You were Matilda? Heh. You've gained a little weight since then!" I went home and cried into a Dairy Queen Blizzard.

At the audition, they had me read the androgynous girl, but apparently wearing a sports bra didn't help, because afterward they asked me to read Sally, her older and more feminine friend. I tried to keep a straight face during the "it's soft" line, but I already suspected I wasn't going to get either part.

My father drove me home, and I wondered why he had even let me audition for it. Usually when a script contained anything he deemed inappropriate, he just outright refused. Maybe he felt like it was important to keep up the appearance of being a working actor, or maybe he already knew I wasn't going to get it.

When we got a script called *Thirteen* a few months later, I knew right away that it was going to offend my father's Republican sensibilities.

"I don't like it," he said. "There's no recovery or redemption at the end. She's just a skank."

"Okay," I said, not sure what to say. There were too many feelings at once: disappointment, bemusement (where had my father learned the word "skank"?), frustration, and even a little relief.

The character had to make out with boys (and with girls), which I hadn't even done in real life. She was supposed to be sexy, or at least seem like she was trying to be sexy. Every time I had tried to be sexy, even jokingly, one of my friends just said, "No, Mara. No."

"Did you look through the sides for that other one?" he said.

"*Catch That Kid*?" I said, incredulous. "It's way too young for me."

"If they really like you, they could change it for you."

"It's been a while since they've done that," I said. There had also been a time when people would just *ask* me to be in a movie, without making me audition, but that didn't happen anymore, either.

"Well, you have to keep trying for stuff if you want to keep acting," he reminded me again.

"I know." When I was alone, I could admit to myself that acting wasn't as fun as it had once been. But I *had* to keep doing it, didn't I? It was the constant in my life. My family had changed, my body had changed, my life had changed. Sometimes it felt like acting was all I had.

He drove me to the *Catch That Kid* audition, staying in the car while I ran inside. As soon as I signed in and looked around, I noticed something was wrong. Every other girl there was at least three years younger than I was. None of them had breasts or braces, like I did. If I had been six years younger, like my sister Anna, I would have fit in better.

Once it was over, I went outside, stomped across the parking lot to my dad's car, threw open the passenger door, climbed in, and slammed the door shut.

"What's the matter with you?" said my father.

"They were all Anna's age!" I said.

"Well, if they like you enough—" he said.

"No," I said. "They won't."

He was quiet. If I had acted this way any other time he would have told me I was being a brat, but I was right, and he knew it.

The part went to an actress three years younger than I was, a sullen but cute tomboy named Kristen Stewart. Her first speaking role had been as a sullen but cute tomboy in *The Safety of Objects*. The next year, she would land another of the few parts I ever actually wanted, Melinda Sordino in the adaptation of Laurie Halse Anderson's book *Speak*. My father and I had met with *Speak*'s director, and I had all but begged for the part. I couldn't understand why I wasn't cast.

I might not have been working hard to prepare for the auditions for scripts I didn't like, but I wasn't getting *any* parts. I always thought it would be me giving up acting, not the other way around.

Something didn't make sense, at least until I was called for a role in a pilot about girls at a boarding school. I would be playing "the fat girl." Just by virtue of being a lazy American teenager, I was probably a few pounds overweight, but I hadn't ever prompted the kind of response this character had. There was a fat joke on every page. I'm not sure if being called for this part said more about me or about the pilot's production team.

"We'd be putting you in big clothes to make you look bigger," the casting director reassured me. It had worked for Jan in *Grease*. I nodded, but what I really wanted to ask was why they hadn't called me in for one of the other characters, like Becca. She was funny and quirky, and constantly changing her personality. She was also neurotic, and while I might have been losing faith in my acting ability, I *knew* I could play neurotic. They didn't ask me to read for her. Then I saw on a shelf a head shot of the most beautiful girl I had ever seen. Right by her name, there was a Post-it note marked "Called back for Becca!"

That's when I understood.

Things had changed. At thirteen, being pretty mattered more than it ever had before—and not just in the world of movies and TV. The prettygirls at school had always had an air of superiority and importance, but once we hit puberty, they *did* seem to matter more. The boys had crushes on them, the girls wanted to be their friends, even the teachers seemed to like them the best. My career was the one thing I had over them. Now that it was waning, I was just another weird, nerdy, loud girl with bad teeth and bad hair whose bra strap was always showing.

Even if I wasn't going to be one of them, I told myself, I could still try to be prettier. The only problem was I didn't know *how.* Before she stopped nannying for us to pursue acting, Shoshanna had given me a rudimentary lesson on how to apply concealer and blush, but I was having to figure out the rest on my own. Every morning in eighth grade I'd put Weezer's upbeat angst anthem "Why Bother?" on repeat and apply pink eyeshadow up to my eyebrows. At least until the day Dana Valdez, a prettygirl who sat next to me in first period, took one disdainful look and said, "Eye shadow goes on your *eyelids.*"

"You're a bitch," I blurted out before I could stop myself.

"Well, I'm a bitch who knows how to put on makeup." She had me there.

Dressing was even harder. My mother, who sometimes drove me to school in her nightgown, had been decidedly uninterested in fashion, and I seemed to have inherited her lack of interest. I had no idea what colors or styles looked good on me, and no one else seemed to know, either: my father's idea of shopping was taking me to Kmart (often to the boys' department), picking out a pair of jeans, and saying, "Do you like these? Good, grab six more pairs and let's go." I thought things would improve when he married my well-dressed stepmother, but she had never had children, so she dressed me the way she dressed herself. As my fashionable, bisexual, fair-weather friend Emily put it, "Mara, you dress like a forty-year-old lesbian."

Auditions were a lost cause. After the Becca incident, I refused

Rocking my dad jeans on the Isle of Man.

69

to take them seriously. Taking them seriously would mean having to face up to the inevitable rejection, having to realize that what I had believed to be the one constant no longer was. Instead, I self-sabotaged. Sometimes it felt out of my control: I would know in my head how the lines should sound, but when they left my mouth, they sounded wrong. Other times it was conscious: a character on a TV show described herself as "flat chested," so, naturally, I wore a push-up bra to the audition. It was a tiny act of rebellion. If I was going to break up with Hollywood, I wanted it to be mutual.

After a year of no callbacks, my father said what we had both been thinking.

"Maybe you should just focus on school right now."

It would mean having to pass up some great scripts I was getting—like an "experimental" comedy series called *Arrested Development*—but it was the right move. I didn't know who I was without film sets, casting directors, and constant rejection, and I needed to find out.

At sixteen, I left the Burbank school system for an arts boarding school called Idyllwild Arts. At Idyllwild I learned about theater history, dramaturgy, directing, and how to write and perform my own work. I wanted to do it all, but I did expect I would go back to film acting at some point. Thinking about life without it made me anxious. But I knew by then that if I wanted to be in film, I had to be beautiful. It would happen, I was sure. It was just going to take a while. For now, I was a teenager and I was still allowed to be awkward. A lot of child actors reappeared after puberty, like butterflies from cocoons, fresh-faced and ready for Neutrogena commercials.

Then, at sixteen, I opened a magazine—likely *Entertainment Twice-a-Fortnight*—and saw a familiar face. Six years earlier, I had met a pretty, friendly twelve-year-old girl with red hair at a press conference on child acting. When a reporter asked if any of us had trouble with the kids at school, she'd said the kids at her middle school had teased her so badly, she had transferred to a special school for child actors and performers. She had done much better there and made lots of friends. It had stuck in my mind; whenever public school was miserable, I reminded myself there were other schools just for people like me, where they'd understand.

After the press conference we all hung out, and I tried to talk to the pretty red-haired girl more. I wanted to ask her what had happened at her school, and how I would know if it had gotten so bad that I should transfer. Instead, I watched her pull a balloon off a display, suck in the helium, and sing, "We're the Chipmunks! C-H-I-P-M-U-N-K-S!" She wasn't in such a serious mood anymore, and it made me like her more. There was something very attractive about her, a kind of cool older-sister vibe, and I wanted to be her friend.

"Dad, I really liked Scarlett," I said to him on our ride home. "Maybe I could . . ." I hunted for words. It was the days after playdates and before "hanging out." "Maybe I could meet up with her sometime?"

"I'm sure you'll see her again," he said.

But I never did. The magazine spread was the first I'd seen of her since. There was Scarlett, looking beautiful, talking about her role in a film with Bill Murray, and she was most definitely a woman. She was in grown-up movies now, being sexy, probably doing that thing where women cross their arms in front of them to take off their shirts. How had she *done* it?

There was a sinking feeling in my stomach. Scarlett was only two or three years older than I was. There was no way I was going to become even half as beautiful as she was in that time. Even after I got my braces off, even if I got contact lenses, even with a better haircut, I was always going to look the way I did, which wasn't beautiful. I knew I wasn't a gorgon, but I guessed that if ten strangers were to look at a photo of me, probably about four or five of them would find me attractive. That would not be good enough for Hollywood, where an actress had to be attractive to eight out of ten people to be considered for even the homely best friend character.

The real world was a bit more forgiving. By this time, plenty of boys were interested in me. True, some of them were *troubled* boys, the kind who'd met their last girlfriends in the psych ward, or wrote poems calling me "sweet" but spelled it like "sweat." And true, often even the ones I liked back had issues. But at least I was finally getting some attention.

It was even easier when I got to college. During my first week of classes I met Sam, a film major with curly dark hair and warm brown eyes. He started walking me back to my dorm after class, and I was surprised by how comfortable I felt around him. The more he laughed at my jokes and told me about himself, the cuter he seemed.

"I wish I could just have a machine that validated me," I told him on one of our walks. "Like I could punch a button and it would say, 'You're not ugly.'"

"I could be that machine," he said, and gestured to his shoulder. "Punch me!"

I did, lightly, and he said, "You're not ugly!" We both laughed, and I punched him again. He told me all the things I was not over and over again, and once we reached Weinstein Hall, he asked me out to the New York Philharmonic.

"You're so cute," Sam told me on our first date, and again on our second, and every time he saw me for the next three years. It was the first time someone had called me cute, and meant it honestly, in years. Each time I'd close my eyes and let it sink in, try my hardest to hold on to what he had said, try not to let it slip. There was something soothing and encouraging in it. I'd built up such a tolerance when I was younger. Now compliments were like methadone.

We fell into a routine together as we fell in love, and I buried myself in our relationship and my classes. But my appearance anxieties were always there underneath, and my past was never gone. I did a "Where Are They Now?" interview for an entertainment TV show, but they never aired it because they said I looked "too pale." I'd pass newsstands on my way to class, clad in pajama pants and one of Sam's shirts, and see my former friends and peers, Lacey Chabert, Hilary Duff, Scarlett Johansson, and, inevitably, Kristen Stewart, on magazine covers, looking immaculate.

It was fine, I told myself. They had always been the pretty girls of the acting world. That was never going to be me anyway. Nobody was ever going to ask me to be on the cover of *Cosmopolitan* or *Maxim*, but I could still have an acting career. Stage acting was much more fun than film anyway, and Chekhov always provided a part for the less attractive actresses. I'd played Sonya from *Uncle Vanya* in a scene for a class, and my acting teacher had told me, "Mara, you need to play this part sometime. She's perfect for you." It might have felt more like a compliment if half of Sonya's lines hadn't been about how plain she was.

"Do you even *want* to be an actor?" asked another teacher. It was a fair question. I tended to freeze up and self-sabotage in acting classes—and that was when I wasn't sleeping through them. I didn't know what I wanted, but whatever it was, I wanted it to be my *choice*. I didn't want to stop acting because I *had* to, because I was too ugly.

"Maybe I should just get plastic surgery," I said to Sam. Sometimes I secretly wished I'd be in an accident where I'd injure my nose and jaw so I could get reconstruction guilt-free. A mirror did fall on my face once, but it left me with only a scar on the bridge of my nose and a feeling that it might have been an omen.

"If you want to, you can," he said, shrugging. Sam had grown up in a well-to-do area of New Jersey where it was typical for insecure girls to get nose jobs as graduation gifts. "But I want you to know I love you the way you are. You're beautiful."

I tried to believe him, but it was as if he were pouring water into a glass with a hole in the bottom. It took a toll on our relationship, and I knew it. In our very last fight before our breakup, he told me, "Mara, the one thing I could never stand about you is how much you put yourself down."

"Well, what am I *supposed* to do?" I yelled. There didn't seem to be a happy medium. Maybe there had been a day at school when they had taught how to accept compliments graciously and how to be confident, rather than constantly vacillating between crushing self-doubt and grandiosity. I must have been out filming that day.

As I saw it, when it came to careers, I had three choices: get cosmetic surgery and go out on auditions for the cute and funny best-friend characters, stay the way I was and go out for the meager character actor roles for young women, or accept myself and give up the idea of a Hollywood film acting career. The discussion was a long time coming, but somewhere inside myself, I had always known what I would do. Being pretty, glamorous, and impervious to rejection, the necessary characteristics of a Hollywood actress, were clearly not my strengths. I thought I would miss film acting, but to my surprise, I never did. Creating and performing my own work, as I had been learning to do, was fulfilling enough. I was always happy to act with friends, or in projects I believed in, but I had no desire to go back to being a full-time film actor. When I thought of Hollywood, of auditions, screen tests, and critics, all I could think of was being judged.

Maybe my obsession with looks was extreme and irrational— a kind of Hollywood-induced body dysmorphic disorder—but it wasn't unfounded. Looks did still matter in the real world. It was the first thing people noticed about me, and, I was beginning to see, the first thing people seemed to notice about *any* woman. The 2008 election happened during my senior year at NYU, and I cringed whenever a pundit mentioned Hillary Clinton's wrinkles or "cankles." There were legitimate criticisms to be made about her, so why was everyone focusing on her looks? Clearly, being "ugly" was the worst sin a woman could commit.

The harshest criticism, I noticed, often seemed to come from other women. I didn't want to be that kind of woman, I decided; it wasn't right to hurt others in a way I'd been hurt. From then on, I vowed, I would never say anything negative about a woman's appearance. It had nothing to do with them as a person, and it wasn't something they could easily change. If I didn't want looks to matter, I would have to stop talking and acting as if they did.

Feminism has been slandered as "a way to give ugly women greater prominence in society." And, in a way, it is: feminism is for ugly women, for beautiful women, for all women. Women of all colors, ages, and shapes. It's about giving people an equal chance regardless of their gender, judging them for what they do instead of what they are. I flirted with calling myself a feminist back in high school, when I stayed up late reading *A Doll's House*, and in college, when I stayed up late reading feminist blogs. But I'd always written it off, said I was a "humanist," said things weren't so bad in most Western countries that it warranted my giving myself a label. Feminism was something we needed in the 1970s, I thought, but it wasn't necessary today. As embarrassing as it is to admit, I didn't take it seriously until I realized it affected me, personally. Even in "developed" societies, I realized, women were seen as worthless if they didn't measure up to a certain standard. And the women I'd once called "prettygirls" didn't have it much better: some men didn't see them as people, but as objects to be collected and controlled, something they deserved or were owed. It wasn't right, and it wasn't the way things should be.

"I think I'm becoming a feminist," I told a friend, and I already felt stronger just for having said it. There was something rebellious in it, and something powerful. Being a feminist meant standing up for myself, having the right to live as I wanted, without a man—the proverbial "Man," or Twentieth Century Fox—deciding my value. If I wanted to stop wearing makeup and adopt my father's purely utilitarian style, I could. If I wanted to learn how to dress nicer and experiment with eye shadow (with guidance this time), I could.

Sometimes, that is what I want. Dressing up became more fun once I learned how to do it, and having control over my appearance makes me feel more confident. And there are things I like about the way I look: my eyes are a pretty mix of green, blue, and gray, and, now that I've had time to get used to them, I'd have to concur with Lucy that boobs *are* fab. It takes a long time to break an old habit, though, and I'm still critical of my appearance, still halfway convinced I'm irredeemably ugly. When fans recognize me and ask to take my picture, I quietly panic. I know I don't photograph well, and I know they're going to put it on the Internet, where not everyone knows I'm funny and charming and generally a decent person, and I can't win them over with my personality. It's out of my control, and I am left feeling small once again.

Every week or so, a well-meaning friend or fan sends me an article about me. Below some variation of "WHAT DO THEY LOOK LIKE NOW?" there is inevitably an unflattering photo of me, and hundreds of comments from people who think I'm ugly.

Some are delighted, schadenfreudic: I was once paid to be cute, but now the child actor curse has caught up to me, and I'm not so cute anymore, am I? Others seem angry. My image belongs to them, to their memories and their imagination, and they aren't happy that I don't match up with what they pictured. This type is the most likely to give advice: I should color my hair, get a nose job, lose twenty pounds, go die in a hole somewhere.

I used to feel compelled to respond. Usually I would just tell whoever posted it that I didn't want to hear it, but once I actually contacted the author of a list of "Ugliest Former Child Actors" to ask her why, as a woman, she was perpetuating a ridiculous beauty standard and punishing other women for the way they looked. She wrote me back immediately to apologize. "I write stupid things on the Internet to pay the bills," she said. "I can't afford integrity."

Typically, though, it's not worth it to argue with them. Now I just sigh, block their accounts, and put the comedian Riki Lindhome's song about being considered plain in Los Angeles, but "Pretty in Buffalo," on repeat. (Except my hometown *is*, effectively, part of Los Angeles, and New York's beauty standards are just as strict, if not more so.)

"What do you expect?" my friends and family say. "Those people are losers." Maybe they're right. Some claim to be "insult comedians"—which, given the freely available easy cruelty on the Internet, seems superfluous to me—but usually the ones who are the most critical seem to be normal people who are deeply unhappy with themselves. They want someone else to tear down, and people like me are considered public domain. To them, I'm not a person, I'm a punch line. I understand that comes with the territory, and that celebrities have a contract with the public: they get to be the target of jealousy and criticism, and sometimes admiration, in exchange for money and recognition. But I let that contract run out a while ago. It is not my job to be pretty, or cute, or anything that someone else wants me to be.

I am all for self-improvement. When I'm not sleeping or procrastinating, I am trying to become a better person. So the next time someone, be they someone in Hollywood or (more likely) someone hiding behind a username, decides to tell me what would make me prettier, I'm going to propose the following: I will meet them in person, but before they offer any suggestions, I will ask them to listen. I will tell them about going through puberty in the public eye after my mother died of cancer. I will tell them how it feels to find a website advertising nude photos of yourself as a twelve-year-old. I will tell them that I've looked at "cute" from both sides now, and that in both cases it just made me miserable. I will tell them how fitting it is that the only real acting I do these days is voice-over, where no one can see me, and that one of the characters I play is literally described as "faceless."

We will talk about the beauty standard, how it's changed throughout history, and how different it is in different countries. We will talk about the fashion industry's exploitation of young models and designers. I will remind them, if they are a woman, how often they are seen as little more than how they look. I will ask them how they have been judged, and how much it hurt. I will tell them how much it hurt to experience that kind of criticism on a macro scale, and how free I feel now that I have chosen not to worry about it.

Finally, I will look them in the eye and tell them how my

mother wanted me to prove myself through my actions and skills, rather than my looks. Now I believe I have, and I am happier than ever.

After all that, if they still insist on telling me how I should look, I will consider taking them on as my stylist.

a letter

Dear Matilda,

I know you don't exist.

I'm writing this to you anyway. Maybe because I read too much Neil Gaiman as a teenager and liked the idea of living archetypes. Or maybe because I feel like you've followed me through my life. You were on my brothers' bookshelves twenty-five years ago, and you were in Times Square two days ago. I've seen you framed in a publisher's office and tattooed on a stranger's leg. I've known you longer than I've known my own sister. You are a part of me.

Maybe you would roll your eyes at that. You did always seem a little no-nonsense.

The first time we met, I was four. I had a virus or one of my regularly scheduled sinus-and-ear infections, and my mother had volunteered to read a book out loud to my brother's class. She couldn't find a babysitter, so she brought me with her, and

I huddled in the back of a fourth-grade classroom as she read aloud from a book with a yellow cover. Her favorite part to perform was Miss Trunchbull, but she had you down perfectly, too.

I should have been sleeping, but I was captivated. Here was a little girl, not much older than I was, who loved books, just like I did, and she was a hero. You had powers, both literal and figurative, and you were determined to right the injustices of the world. I loved you. I wanted to be you.

My brothers had your book, and one of them was always reading or rereading it. Once I learned to read a few months later, I would read it over their shoulders.

"Joel! Watch this!" I would say. "'We always watch the telly!' Remember? From *Matilda*?" I knew that impressions were funny, but didn't yet understand that to make someone laugh I would need to quote an actual funny line.

Your book was my favorite. There weren't many other girl characters I could look up to. Even the ones I loved had limited power: Lisa Simpson could be obnoxiously self-righteous sometimes, and Betsy Ray never did manage to win the Deep Valley High School writing contest. You used your wit and brains to outsmart your cruel, superficial parents, and the monstrous head of your school. You were smart, thoughtful, and rebellious in all the right ways. You were what my mother wanted me to be. You were always in the back of my mind.

I had been acting for a year and a half when I encountered you again. My agent Bonnie called my mother one day and said, "There's so much for Mara!"

"Like what?" said my mother. I had enough of a name then that she could be picky with scripts. She didn't want anything rated R or too cute, and though she loved animals, she detested horrible "animal movies."

"Well," said Bonnie, "there's this romantic comedy, there's a horror movie, there's *Matilda*, there's a remake of—"

"Wait, back up," said my mother. "Did you say *Matilda*?"

"You'll never guess what I have," she told me the next day after school, and handed over the script.

"Oh my gosh!" I said when I saw the title, and took it to my room and curled up on my bed, as I did with my favorite books. My mother told me she could hear me laughing over my sister's baby monitor as I read. When I was done, I hugged the script to my chest; I had never wanted to play a character so badly. Other parts were easy come, easy go, but I *had* to play you.

I auditioned with Danny DeVito a few weeks later. He was only about a foot taller than I was, but I wouldn't have been intimidated even if he'd been a giant. He was so warm and avuncular, and he talked to me like I was a person. We ran lines, and then he asked me about my life and school.

"I knew I wanted you for Matilda the moment you walked in," he told me later.

We got the news while doing preproduction for *Miracle* in Chicago. It was Oscar night, and I was on the hotel couch, trying not to fall asleep before Best Picture, when the phone rang.

"Mara, you got it!" my mother said when she hung up. I hadn't heard her that excited in a long time.

"Got what?" I said, sleepily.

"*Matilda!* You're Matilda!"

Nearly a year went by before we started filming, but Danny DeVito and I met a few times in the interim. The day we were supposed to meet with him at the Four Seasons in Beverly Hills, I had a 103-degree fever and my mother had to prop me up so I could talk to him. We saw each other again at the 1995 Golden Globes, and he waved to me when I was onstage with Victor Borge presenting Best Score.

"Danny DeVito called last night," my brother Danny told us a few days later. He tried to imitate his Jersey accent, but just started to laugh. "I swear, at first I thought it was one of my friends doing the Jerky Boys!"

He was in awe, and so were the rest of us. Something was starting to feel different. My other roles hadn't felt like a big deal. This one was.

That March, Danny DeVito welcomed me to preproduction and introduced me to the rest of the cast. Embeth Davidtz was as sweet and lovely as anyone would have expected Miss Honey to be, but the real surprise was Miss Trunchbull, Pam Ferris. At our first meeting, she showed me and Embeth pictures of cats she had rescued, which made me love her immediately. When we started reading, they were both exactly how I had imagined the characters.

The other films I had done had been good experiences, but I had always felt a little peripheral. I was a kid, and no one needed my input. But Danny was different. He sought my creative involvement from the very beginning.

"What do you think we should do for Matilda's powers?" he asked me during preproduction. "A certain look?" We practiced a few looks and squints and head tilts until we settled on one. We called it the Whammy.

With Danny DeVito on set.
I still have my Matilda *hat.*

A few weeks later, he asked, "Do you think Matilda might have some kind of doll she made from the stuff around the house?"

It did seem like something you'd do. "Sure!" I said, and went home that night and drew a doll with red pipe cleaner hair, star button eyes, and patches from newspapers where you might have run out of cloth. Her name, I decided, was Wanda Zinnia Wild. Danny loved her. An art director took my design and tried to make her a little more easy to make, but Danny looked at the drawings side by side and said, "No, I don't want yours, I want *hers*." He found some artists who worked in Claymation and models, and we made Wanda a reality. I had my first design credit at age seven.

Danny had told me that during one scene he wanted me to dance around giving everything the Whammy. Initially, I wasn't sure how I felt about it. I've never been a good dancer. One of my teachers at Idyllwild later told me I was "dead from the neck down," and he might have been right: I've always expressed my emotions with my face rather than my body. This usually wasn't a problem in film, where a close-up on a face can say everything, but now I was anxious.

"Danny," I told him as the filming got closer, "I'm a little nervous about the dance scene."

"Okay, here's the plan, then," he said. "That day, *everyone* on set has to dance. Everyone. It'll be the rule. We'll have a dance party."

And we did. Danny was dancing around yelling, "Whammy that lamp! Whammy the cards!" My mother was dancing, the ADs were dancing, the hair and makeup artists were dancing, even Wanda had been rigged up to dance. But we didn't use "Little Bitty Pretty One" like in the movie—we used a version of Harry Belafonte's "Matilda," which, to me, felt more fitting.

People sometimes think the line where I say "Dahl's chickens" instead of "Charles Dickens" was a mistake they left in, but it was written into the script, a nod to your creator, Roald Dahl. We also called Miss Honey's doll "Lissy," after his wife, Felicity. You would probably appreciate all the little things I learned about him. Lucy Dahl, his daughter, was on set most of the time. She was working on a book called *Matilda's Movie Diary*, as a companion to the film. She interviewed me about my experiences behind the scenes, and I became friends with her daughters. She told us her (your?) father had told them stories about the Big Friendly Giant every night, then climbed up on a ladder outside their window and pretended to blow dreams into their ears, just like the BFG does in the book.

*Being strapped to the bottom of a table
for the Trunchbull house scene.*

"We always thought it really was the BFG," she said.

"How did you figure out it wasn't?" I said.

"He fell off the ladder one night when he'd had a bit too much wine, and we all went to look."

Our conversations led me to suspect that Miss Trunchbull was based partly on Lucy's boarding school headmistress. As Lucy told it, she was a giant, intimidating woman, and one with creative punishments. Lucy and a friend had once tried to hide ice cream from the kitchens in their pajamas and sneak it back into their dorm late at night, but the headmistress caught them. She marched them back into her office and made them stand still until dawn, while the melted ice cream ran down their arms and legs.

"And she just sat there the whole time, knitting."

Working on *Matilda* wasn't always fun—I got really sick of

staring at things endlessly while they took shots from different angles, and I once almost literally got sick after eating waffles with syrup for three hours. But most of the time it *was* fun. There were so many kids on set for me to play with, so many that every now and then I'll introduce myself to someone and they'll say "Oh, we've met before, I was an extra in *Matilda*." Kiami/Lavender and I had secret codes and taught each other hand games. We had a group that would go to a playground and then out to dinner after set, and Liam/Charlie (Who Gets Thrown Out the Window) would always embarrass us by bugging the waitress for a nonalcoholic margarita. Throwing stuff at Pam/Trunchbull as she left Crunchem Hall Academy was a childhood fantasy come true: we got to throw food and make a mess and no one cared! They encouraged it! In one of the last shots, I'm hugging Jacqueline/Amanda (Who Gets Thrown by Her Pigtails) and jumping up and down out of pure joy, completely out of character. We were always told not to hug so much because we would ruin our makeup, but right then we didn't care.

Filming the montage at the end just felt like bonding time with Embeth. We did the dishes to Bob Marley's "Three Little Birds," and actually did have a picnic during the picnic scene. The only thing that didn't go smoothly was when we were supposed to be eating chocolates: Danny was directing us, saying, "Take another! Take two! Laugh!" and then he yelled, "Feed each other!" I glanced down at the perfect chocolate cream I had chosen and tried not to look reluctant as I reached to Embeth. She reached out with hers, I took a bite, and sickeningly sweet cherry cordial spilled down my chin and onto my wardrobe. Everyone laughed, and even though it was gross, I did, too. That was also the day Danny taught me the wonders of a "spit bucket."

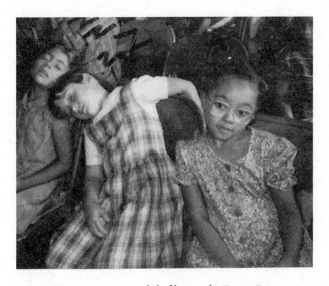

Trying to get some rest while filming the Bruce Bogtrotter cake scene. It took so long to film that instead of putting a start and end time on the call sheet, they just put an infinity symbol.

Danny and his wife, Rhea (who also played my parents), always felt more like my fun uncle and aunt than my boss and coworker. They took me to see *Beauty and the Beast* at the Shubert Theatre and I was welcome at their house whenever I felt like it. And I loved it there: they had a trampoline, a pool and hot tub, a pinball machine, a tiny movie theater in a guesthouse, amazing food at any time of day or night, a room dedicated just to art projects, all kinds of pets, and, best of all, three secret passageways. It was a kid's paradise, and something of a refuge at a time when I really needed it. The weekend my mother had a mastectomy, Danny and Rhea let me sleep over at their place, and I had so much fun I completely forgot she was in the hospital.

And I'll never forget what they did for my birthday.

"They didn't put it on the call sheet," I had told my mother the night before, feeling dejected. "They put 'Happy Birthday, Pam' when it was her birthday, and she wasn't even working that day."

"I'm sure they'll be doing something," she said.

"Are *you* going to do something?" I asked her, a little shyly. The year before she had tied balloons around my bedroom door-knob so it would be the first thing I saw when I woke.

"Mara, I'm really tired." She sighed. She had been going through chemotherapy and was weak and exhausted. "And you shouldn't expect that kind of thing every year."

I went to bed feeling a little disappointed. I woke up to signs telling me to go to the family room, then the living room, then the kitchen, where a bag full of presents was set on the table. My mother had organized a scavenger hunt! She had been sick and tired, but she still wanted to surprise me. It was just beginning: as soon as we pulled into the Sony lot, I saw balloons, hundreds of balloons, stretched in a rainbow arc above my trailer. Inside were boxes with American Girl insignia. Danny and Rhea had given me a Molly doll, and every accessory for her. (I think I had always secretly wanted Samantha, the pretty and wealthy Victorian girl, but I have to admit that Molly, the bespectacled war-era prankster, was definitely more my style.)

There was a Ben & Jerry's sundae cart, and at lunch, a giant chocolate cake in the shape of a red ribbon. The cast and crew sang to me, and I gave Danny a hug in front of everyone. The day ended early so I could go home, celebrate with my family, and plan a party that weekend for all my friends. I can't remember a birthday when I have ever felt more loved.

Matilda took longer than any other film I worked on, but I didn't mind. We started May 8, a date I remember every year, and my last day was a week before Halloween. Some of my friends who grew up on sitcoms say finishing the series felt like leaving their lives behind. Finishing *Matilda* felt more like leaving summer camp. At the end, I had happy memories and lifelong friends. I never thought of how it would change my life, or that I might come to resent you.

There might have been a moment when I thought that you, as a character, were mine. That I got to *be* you, the way I wanted to when I first heard of you. It did not last very long.

I don't remember when I realized it. Admittedly, I don't remember much of 1996, and what I do remember is painful. My mother was gone, my world had changed, and I felt unmoored. The filming of *Matilda* felt like it had happened in another lifetime, or in a dream. Ironically, it was during this time, after I'd finished playing you, that I related to you most. You knew what it was like to feel alone.

It took me a while to get through it. When I came out the other side, I felt as if I'd been replaced. Everyone knew you. Everyone loved you. I had never thought of what would happen when the movie came out, and didn't expect the slow-burn cult following *Matilda* would build over the years. At one point there was a *doll* made of me/you. I didn't think it looked like me at all, though I guess it would have been creepier if it had.

I wished I could have just felt proud. But it wasn't how I was wired, and it wasn't how I was raised. My parents wanted me to be modest—the motto in our household was "The only stars are in the sky"—but, predictably, I took it to the extreme. I thought being confident was being conceited. I couldn't just be happy with what I had done. I didn't know what to do. If I refused to talk about *Matilda*, I was being ungrateful. If I did talk about it, I was bragging, which seemed worse. For years, I didn't mention you at all, but you kept following me.

I knew the truth, that a lot of actors aren't nearly as interesting as the people they portray. Whenever someone brought you up, I would get the same twinge in my stomach I got when someone praised my brothers for getting straight A's. You might as well have been my twin. People were always getting me and you confused, and I knew everyone loved you much more than they loved me. A boy at camp said, "I liked you more before I knew you." (To be fair, I had been pretty moody that summer.) Girls would show up at my door after midnight when I was at NYU because they wanted to party with Matilda. I've lost count of how many times people came up to me and asked, "Is your name Matilda?" I always said no, because it isn't. "Are you Matilda?" was similarly troubling. I didn't feel comfortable saying yes. It felt disrespectful to both of us.

As uncomfortable as it might have been, there was always a part of me that missed you. But I grew up, and you didn't. I wanted to grow up. I wanted to be Mara, but everyone knew me as Matilda. You wouldn't let me go. What if you were all there was to me?

If I could talk to you, maybe you would understand. If you had grown up, I wonder if you would have ever felt like you peaked, like you couldn't top what you accomplished when you were little. In the book, you lost your powers. In the movie, you chose not to use them as much. I guess I did a little of both.

* * *

A few years ago, I heard about a new musical adaptation of your book being staged in London's West End. People kept asking me about it, and I felt pained. I knew you weren't mine anymore, that you hadn't really ever been, and I had thought I was okay with that. But I didn't realize how much I had missed you. Still, I saw it when it came to Broadway, and I thought it was great. The music was wonderful, heartfelt, funny, and catchy. The actors were all so talented, and Oona Laurence was such an adorable Matilda, I wanted to run up onstage and hug her. It was a beautifully staged show, and the audience loved it. When it was over, I gave a standing ovation, along with the rest of the house. Leaving the auditorium, I wondered, a bit self-consciously, if anyone would recognize me.

Nobody did, and to my own surprise, I felt a little sad. This was a surprise: I hadn't wanted to be recognized for years. When I was young and first getting stopped and asked for autographs, sometimes I felt so overwhelmed that I would just pretend to be someone else ("Nope, I'm just Katie from Chicago, but I get that a lot"). As I got older, it stopped happening as often, but when it did, it always seemed to happen when I was feeling and looking ill, or when I was in some other compromised state. TSA agents always asked me, "Are you that girl from that movie?" right as I was scrambling to get my belt and shoes back on, and once a phlebotomist asked me while she drew my blood. (This seems to be common among the formerly famous. I once asked Jonathan Lipnicki the most awkward time he'd been recognized. He told me, "I once had a nurse ask me if I was the little kid from *Jerry Maguire* while she was pulling out my catheter." He wins. Or loses.) I hated them seeing me—not Matilda, but Mara—at my worst. I was afraid to disappoint them, and I always believed I would. What should have been a nice honor became an embarrassment. I think being recognized, to me, was what having the waiters sing to you in a restaurant on your birthday is to everyone else.

I had wanted to be me and not you. I hadn't appreciated it enough. Now it was as if the part of me that felt like you was gone. Now you belonged to someone else—four other little girls, in fact—and it felt bittersweet. I've been labeled "bitter" before: it's hard for some people to understand feeling more than one thing, especially people on the Internet. My relationship with you, a fictional little girl, is the most complicated relationship I'll likely ever have.

Seeing the musical may have been cathartic for me. It helped me realize you don't belong to me. *Matilda* is a tradition. My brothers passed the book on to me. My therapist told me her daughters love it. I've seen the book and movie name checked on feminist sites and in preteen girls' magazines. There's another generation embracing you now. You are such a beloved character, and so inspirational to so many people. How could I ever have expected you to be limited to only one interpretation?

A few months after seeing the musical, I met Sophia Gennusa, one of the Broadway Matildas, at a Roald Dahl–themed charity event. She was adorable and gave a great performance of the song

"Naughty" (which I totally have on my phone—it's a great song!). She had that same steady gaze and mischievous smile I had when I was her age. I went up to her after she came offstage and started to say, "Hi, I'm Mara," but her equally adorable mother blurted out, "Oh yeah, we know who you are!" I laughed, and felt heartened as we all took a picture together.

Later that year I got an e-mail from Danny DeVito. He and I had lost contact after I went away to school, but he found a way to get in touch and asked if I wanted to be in a *Matilda* reunion to celebrate the Blu-ray release. I said yes.

I stayed in Danny and Rhea's amazing house. Pam Ferris was staying in a guesthouse nearby, and she was as lovely as ever. She showed me pictures of her rescue dog, told me about being in one of my favorite movies, *Children of Men*. We actually ended up getting a little drunk together at a restaurant on Melrose, which is not something I ever expected to happen.

Before I went to bed that night, Danny and I talked about my mother. *Matilda* was easily the movie I'd made that she was most excited about, but she had died while we were doing postproduction. I'd always felt sad that she wasn't able to see the completed film.

I was floored when he told me he'd brought my mother the film while she was in the hospital. It hadn't been fully edited, but she had been able to see what we had. I feel such a sense of peace knowing that, and I'll always be grateful to Danny for it. You, and your story, were a part of her life until the very end.

And you'll always be a part of me, too. A month before the reunion I was at my brother's wedding in Savannah, Georgia. Savannah is

In the Everglades for a charity event,
a month after we wrapped Matilda.

basically a smaller New Orleans, a friendly party city where you can drink on the street and strangers will tell you stories about the ghosts haunting their houses. We went to a dive bar after the wedding—though for a dive bar, it was pretty classy: Jimmy Carter had announced his candidacy for president there! (My father might insist that makes it *less* classy.) My sister beat everyone at darts, and we talked with Savannah's locals, like a man who led ghost tours, and a guy who had a cat on a leash. I was sipping champagne out of a plastic cup and bouncing—not dancing—along to the blaring jukebox when a man came up to me.

"Excuse me, I'm sorry to bother you, but are you the girl who was in *Matilda*?"

"Yes, I am," I said, smiling.

"Oh, wow! My wife—she's sitting right over there," he said, gesturing to a shy-looking woman in a booth. "Well, that movie means a lot to her."

"I'm so glad to hear that," I said, and I was.

His voice got quieter. "See, it was her niece's favorite movie, and her niece passed away last year."

"Oh no," I said. "I'm so sorry."

"I know, it's been hard. . . . If you have a second, do you think you could sit and talk with her?"

"Of course." The woman in the booth was wiping away tears as I walked over to her. She took my hand and told me about her niece, how much *Matilda* had meant to her, and how seeing me brought back memories of her. We cried and hugged, and she asked me how I was liking Savannah.

"It's wonderful! My brother just got married tonight," I said, pointing out him and his wife.

"Oh, they're a beautiful couple." She sighed. Her husband came up, all smiles, and offered to buy the entire wedding party drinks and songs on the jukebox. We ended up celebrating with them all night.

I will always remember the look on that woman's face and what you meant to her. It was something I can, and will, always take pride in. It's moments like that which make me feel grateful— meeting fans who say Matilda gave them hope, seeing posts on Tumblr about how heartening it was to see a movie where a girl is celebrated for being smart and working hard—I had forgotten how much power you have. You empower people. You always have. You give hope to those who feel lost. You showed those whose families didn't understand them that they could make their own, the way you made yours with Miss Honey. You were, and still are, revolutionary. I don't care if you'd roll your eyes at that. It's the truth, and I've seen it.

I hope you know, to me, you're always family.

Love,
Mara

goddess oracle

It's one in the morning and my sister is reading my cards.

"Do you have a thought or intention, or do you just want a general read?"

"Just general, I guess." I'm on my couch in New York; Anna's in her rented room in a house in the Bay Area. Anna knows I don't believe in signs or "holding space" or "energy" like she does, but she knows I like it when she reads my cards. It makes her happy, which makes me happy. And if I'm being honest, sometimes I do see a connection between the cards and something in my life—not because the cards are right, of course, but because they force me to reflect. To focus. To Anna, though, it's different; it's sacred.

The two of us do everything over Skype. We talk about the weird things we saw that day in our respective cities. I defend my love for Nicki Minaj and Lady Gaga, and she defends her love for Rihanna and Taylor Swift. She oil paints while I bake cookies. I paint my nails while she makes dinner. Sometimes we do these things in silence, happy just to see each other. Sometimes we fight, but usually not. Our worst fights always seem to happen when we see each other in person, and for some reason it's always the night before one of us has to leave.

My favorite defining Anna moment happened on a night we were doing yoga together via Skype.

"Mara, there's this YouTube link that says 'Yoga, for Menstruation, for *Men*.'"

"That . . . doesn't make sense," I said. "You're misreading it."

"No, it really does say that! I'll screenshot it!" she said, calling for her roommate to come over and verify it.

"Then it's a typo," I said. "Or a prank. Some kind of sexist joke."

"Yeah, or maybe it's for transgender people, or maybe—oh, I know what it is," she said. "I have this extension on my browser called Jailbreak the Patriarchy, and it randomly switches 'he' and 'she' or 'man' and 'woman.'"

"That," I would later tell my friends, "is my sister in a nutshell." There are other stories I could tell: her stopping phone conversations with me to fawn over puppies she passes on the street; befriending the Jehovah's Witnesses who proselytize at her BART station; arguing that the most heroic video game character ever was Paperboy ("I would NEVER, ever take such a horrible job with runaway tires and spooky houses and weird gargoyle things and keep doing it day after day!"); or having synesthesia so strongly she gets a headache if something is written in the "wrong" color. It's all so *her*.

Anna was almost born in San Francisco. She should have been. Then we'd be able to explain why Anna is the way she is: a born artist; a wide-eyed, sensitive but passionate, whimsical flower child from birth.

Our mother was eight months pregnant with her when we first went up there to do preproduction on *Doubtfire*. But she went home to have her, leaving me in the care of my father. It didn't seem to bother her so much that he wouldn't be there when she gave birth, or for the first few weeks of the new baby's life. She and my father loved each other deeply, but she didn't need him. After four kids, delivering a fifth was like having a dentist appointment, uncomfortable but familiar.

My parents were so casual about it by that point, we didn't even have a name for her for the first month of her life. Whenever people would gush over her and ask her name, my brother told me, there would be a long silence before one of them would say, "Uh, Nina," or, "Uh, Gabrielle," or whatever name our parents were leaning toward that week.

To be fair, for the first week of my life I didn't have a name, either. It was between "Mara" and "Laura," until finally my mother's Jewish guilt kicked in and the more Jewish-sounding one won. (The name means "of eternal beauty" in Gaelic, but my parents named me the Hebrew one, which means "bitter." Being bitter was my birthright.) For my sister, we eventually settled on Anna, as long as we promised our mother we'd never call her "Anna Banana." "Anna" was simple and pretty, and it means "grace."

On a rainy April day in 1993, I flew from San Francisco to Burbank to meet my sister, already knowing I loved her. Our mother would ask me on the phone if I wanted to talk to the baby, and I'd coo at her until my mom took the phone back and promised me the baby was smiling in her sleep. I couldn't wait to meet her. For as long as I could remember I had wished for a little sister, and now that I had one, she was going to be my new built-in best friend. She had no choice in the matter.

The first time I saw her, asleep in a tiny pink hat, I was not disappointed: she was adorable, and I adored her. No one would ever understand how much. In every picture from that time, I'm cuddling her so tightly she looks uncomfortable. I gave her so many kisses on her little face that when she got strong enough, she reached up and pushed me away.

We lied to Southwest Airlines about the baby's age so she could fly with us back to San Francisco while I finished filming. We stayed together for the next three months, just us girls. One

Danny, Joel, Jon, me, and baby Anna on the steps of my Mrs. Doubtfire *trailer.*

of our mother's hands was always in mine, and the other was holding Anna. She was a tiny woman, but she never seemed to get tired from holding or carrying us. Anna still seemed like a part of our mom, but so was I. I never knew where she ended and I began.

Back in the present, Anna's shuffling my cards.

"Goddess oracle, light the way . . . what does the universe have in store for Mara today?" She fans them out in front of the camera. "Pick one."

I point to one on the left side. Anna turns it toward herself.

"Oh, I never know how to pronounce this one. If . . . Iffy-Jenny-ah?" She turns it toward me.

"Iphigenia." It's a name I know both from Greek tragedies and from *Doubtfire*.

"Right! Wait, is this . . . Is she the one who . . ." She scours the fine print. "Wow, that's an intense card." Anna looks back at me. "She was sacrificed, right?"

"Yeah, but it's more complicated than that."

"More complicated than human sacrifice?"

"Well, some people say she *wanted* to be sacrificed," I say.

Anna chews her cheek and opens her interpretation book. She lays the card down on her bed. It shows a young woman looking off into the sea, facing her fate.

On a March day in 1995, our mother told me my grandfather was coming over with his camera, and we were going to take some pictures out in the backyard.

"Pictures of me?" I said.

"You, me, and Anna."

"Do I have to?" This was during post-*Miracle* publicity blitz, right after the Golden Globes and the Oscars, where I'd performed in the opening number alongside Tim Curry. I was tired of having my photo taken, and in the past few months, I'd become used to getting my way.

"Mara, I really think you should." She had a strange look on her face.

"Mom, I don't want to."

"I want you to." I didn't understand why she was pressuring me. She hated having her picture taken.

"But I really don't want to!"

"Mara, will you please just do it so that even if I have cancer, and all my hair falls out, you'll still have a picture of me looking normal?" She started crying.

My breath had gone. "Mom, what . . . what are you talking about?"

"I might . . . I have breast cancer."

I don't know what I said to her after that, only that I agreed to pose for the photos.

I've never forgotten what our mother's voice sounded like, or what she thought and felt, but sometimes I can't remember exactly what she looked like. So many of my memories are of her looking the way she did when she was sick. The picture of us my grandfather took that day, the last time she looked healthy, was in my bedroom for years. Me, my sister, and our mother, all wearing red, all with shoulder-length hair, smiling in the sunshine.

"The book says this card is about accepting your destiny," Anna says.

"I can see that, I guess," I say. "But I don't know that it applies to my life."

"It'll come to you," Anna says. Then she says, "It's getting so long."

She's talking about her hair. My sister and I have the same roundabout, digressive, all-over-the-place way of talking, jumping from A to B to Z and then back to C and D. Sometimes my friends get confused, but Anna always gets it, and I always get her.

Her grown-out pixie cut is finally long enough for her to pull into two little ponytails. "It looks good either way," I say.

"Dad hates my hair short," she says. "You should have seen him when I said I wanted to shave my head. He got really freaked out."

"Dad's old-fashioned," I say. The one man who came of age in the sixties and seventies without ever having touched pot.

"It's not that," she says. "He has this thing, I think. Something about women with no hair. It really bugs him. You know?"

I didn't know that, but I nod. It makes sense.

Our mother didn't like wigs. When she started losing her hair, she wore scarves and hats to cover her head, if she wore anything. The first week of *Matilda* preproduction, Danny DeVito saw her wearing a flowered floppy hat straight out of *Blossom* and joked, "Who does your mom think she is, wearing a hat like that?" I looked to her, not knowing what to say, but she just smiled politely. She hadn't told him yet.

She had a sense of humor about her illness. She'd let me pet the soft hair that grew in after she'd stopped her first round of chemo. I once took a Polaroid of her lifting her hat up slightly, seductively, the Gypsy Rose Lee of the UCLA Medical Center oncology ward. She bought a silicon insert to even out her bra after her mastectomy, and was known to reach down and throw it onto the table when conversations got dull. Even as her health declined, it was hard to take her illness too seriously. She wanted to be strong, and she wanted us to see her as strong. And we did.

My sister and I both knew she was sick, though I knew more than Anna did—she was six years younger than me, and I was only eight. After her mastectomy, I knew she'd had an operation. Anna did not. Our mother was in her bedroom one day, with the door unlocked, draining the wound and painting it with iodine, when Anna burst in. From the other side of the house, I heard screaming, and ran to the source.

The room smelled like iodine. Our mother was sitting on her bed, topless. Anna was in her arms, shaking, her face wet with tears.

"She saw the tubes and freaked out," our mother said with a sigh.

I wanted to say, "Tubes? What tubes?" I didn't know what she meant. But I just nodded.

From then on, whenever our mother cleaned her stitches she locked the door, and we told Anna, "Mommy's painting herself."

There were times after our mother died when someone reminded me of her. Women of Eastern European heritage with thick dark hair and low voices, like our mother's, unnerved me. Watching Jane Kaczmarek on *Malcolm in the Middle* was uncanny, and it was even more uncomfortable when I saw her in person at an awards show. I once stood in front of a WANTED sign for five minutes because a woman who was wanted for kidnapping had our mother's glasses.

Mostly, though, I didn't think of her. We hardly ever even said her name out loud. It was as if she hadn't existed.

"Missing Mom?" a teacher who'd known her asked me a few months after. I nodded, but the truth was I wasn't. I was trying not to think of her at all.

It would come to me in the rare moments I was alone. When my guard was down. I cried all night after the *Rugrats* Mother's Day special. "Mother Simpson," with Homer sitting on his car during the credits, staring off into the night, pained me so much I couldn't cry. TV betrayed me. For years I knew, but didn't know, why even the happy episodes of *Gilmore Girls* left me aching.

At age thirteen I tried to read *Motherless Daughters*, Hope

Edelman's book on growing up after one's mother leaves or dies, but I couldn't get through the first chapter. It hurt too much. Ten years later I tried again, with a pencil and a highlighter. Most of the book is underlined, dog-eared, or bright yellow. My life made sense, narratively. I was eight when our mother died, in the "concrete operational stage," when kids are still delineating what is real and what is not. "Some therapists believe," I highlighted, "that the children who lose a parent during this time have the hardest time coping."

"Do you want me to do another reading, from my goddess deck?" Anna asks now.

"I thought this was your goddess deck," I say.

"No, this was my 'heroines and feminine archetypes' deck," she says. "I just say 'goddess oracle' because it sounds good." I feel stupid—of course Iphigenia wasn't a goddess.

"I love this deck," Anna says, bringing the goddess deck out and shuffling it. "The cards are so beautiful. Do you want to see my favorites?"

I nod, and she pulls out three. "Here's Kwan Yin, here's Mary Magdalene, and here's the Virgin Mary. Aren't they beautiful?"

"They are."

"Pick one," Anna says again. I do and she looks at it. "Oooh, you got Aphrodite!"

"What does that mean?" I say. It could have something to do with the man I had dinner with on Thursday, but that seems too obvious.

"How was it?" Anna had asked me earlier.

"Good," I'd said, listing a few of his good qualities. "And also, well . . . His dad died, so . . . So he *knows*. You know?"

"Right." We've both had a kinship with other people whose parents died when they were young. It's especially strong with other women whose mothers died. I call us "the saddest sorority."

No one knows what to say to a child when a parent dies. In a best-case scenario, the child will know it's okay for them to feel whatever they feel. But no one mentions how it will affect the rest of his or her life. No one told me I'd spend the rest of my life living with a ghost.

What I felt most, at the time, was anger. Whatever gentle qualities I'd had seemed to die with our mother. At recess, I started leaving behind the well-meaning girls who pitied and tried to empathize with me in favor of roughhousing with the boys, who would tease me until I would chase after them and fight with them.

The one person I could be gentle with was my baby sister. She was so little and so vulnerable. We shared a room, and every night I wasn't away on a set or at camp, I'd tuck her in a second time after our father left, and sing her "Someone to Watch over Me" like our mother had. Sometimes I'd fall asleep in her trundle bed, the way our mother used to when the chemo had tired her out too much, but usually I'd go back to my bed and lie awake worrying about her. I sensed even then that she couldn't quite communicate all she was thinking and feeling. I was angry and I felt crazy, but there was no way of knowing what was happening inside her.

I did not want to be pitied. Pity reminded me I was weak. But I pitied Anna. A memory played again and again in my mind, of when our mother said good night to her for the last time. My baby sister had responded, "Okay, Mommy. See you in the morning."

"You keep acting like Anna's *mother*," one of my brothers yelled at me in a fight when I was nine. He only said it once, but it left me with a deep feeling of shame. It made me feel as if I'd committed a kind of blasphemy.

It wasn't like I was the only one who was there for her. We had our father and a bevy of nannies. Then there was the Greek chorus of teenage boys—our brothers and their friends—who were always around, looking out for us. Eventually, there was our stepmother. But Anna and I were always together. Even when we were alone, we had each other. Or perhaps it's more accurate to say I had *her*. I may have needed her even more than she needed me.

We always knew Anna would be an artist. When she was a baby, she made perfectly symmetrical patterns with her blocks, and by the time she was six, every piece of paper in the house was covered with crayon drawings of pretty girls in dresses, and cartoon frogs. Sometimes I would make up stories and she would illustrate them. Our greatest collaboration was a comic book about romance and teenage vampires (something we lamented never cashing in on after the *Twilight* craze). We were collaborators as well as best friends, and we were completely inseparable. "Bestsister-friends," I called us. Everyone else in our family spoke of us as a unit, "The Girls."

When I went away to boarding school—putting up so many

of Anna's cartoon drawings in my room that a fellow student said, "Wow, you *really* like bunnies"—she was left alone. I told myself it wouldn't be a big deal; she had gotten used to our brothers being away at college, and she was used to me being gone for months at a time to film. This was different, though. She was only ten, and she'd never been the only child living at home before. When I went to NYU, it was even harder: I was a five-hour plane ride away instead of a two-hour car ride. She started referring to our childhood, half-jokingly, as "Before you abandoned me." It gutted me. I would remind her that she could call me at any time, and made her promise to send me more cartoons and letters. I didn't miss home, but I missed her.

I never thought we would grow apart, but we did. In the days before I started my Twitter, I kept a list of one-liners as a Word file—in a folder called "You Think You're Funny." I let Anna read it once when I came home for the holidays. She looked more and more serious as she went on. I started getting nervous. Anna, under my stepmother's tutelage, was going through a conservative religious phase, and she could be judgmental. Maybe my jokes were a little darker and more risqué than I remembered.

"Wow," Anna said when she finished. She was chewing her cheek, like she did when she was trying to figure something out.

"What?"

"You know, Mara, I think I've kind of always assumed we were, like, the same person." She spoke rapidly, not looking me in the eye. "And now, some of this stuff, it's just . . . different, and I realize you're a different person, you know, and we're not."

"Oh. Well, what was it?" Maybe the line about a guy being so cute I was afraid to talk to him sober? "Was it the drinking stuff? Because I'm not, like, an alcoholic, I don't drink that much, that was just a one-off joke. And, I mean, I'm twenty-two, it's not a big deal if I drink."

Anna shrugged. She hadn't known where she ended and I began, but I had shown her.

"It says one of the best ways to honor Aphrodite is by dancing," Anna says. "Don't you love that?"

"No one wants to see me dance," I say.

"Who cares?" she says. But she's a great dancer, naturally graceful. As my brother Jon once said, "Anna got the dancing gene. Mara did not."

"Maybe you need to dance more," she says. "Maybe that's what the card is about. Expression."

"I get paid to express myself," I say, which is a bit of a stretch. I'm not sure writing the odd blog post or freelance article when I'm not working at my nonprofit day job or babysitting is really "expression."

She's changed since she first read my jokes, become more open-minded, but I still get nervous when I talk to Anna about my work. I love the way her mind works; I've always admired her art, and I want her to appreciate what I do. Sometimes I wish she'd ask me for stories again, like I used to tell her when we were kids. But she's grown up now. She can't remember the days when we were alone together, when I ran her baths, gave her the soft tissues she liked when she was sick, sang her the same bedtime songs our mother had sung to us. She doesn't know how hard I tried to take care of her. I can't fault her for it, but still, sometimes I'm sad that she can't remember all our little moments together.

"Are you still thinking of moving out here?" she says.

"Maybe. Probably not anytime soon, though."

"You should do it now, before the bro-grammers take over."

Every time I visit Anna, I'm overwhelmed with memories. I'll sit on Telegraph Hill or on a bench in Embarcadero, look out onto the bay, and start to cry. I never want to leave. San Francisco is the last place I was a kid. Before I was famous, before I had responsibilities, back when all my worries were just hypothetical. Where our mother bought a copy of *Eloise* and wrote "For Mara, who is living life at the St. Francis hotel" on the inside cover. Where it was just us. It's where she feels the most real to me. So many other times she seems like a figure in a dream I had a long time ago.

When a person is gone, all that's left is a narrative. At some point, that narrative becomes myth. If there's one thing I regret, it's letting our mother's death overshadow her life.

I chew my cheek. "I think I know what it is," I say. "Iphigenia. I haven't been very good at facing my responsibilities lately, because I've been too scared, so maybe this is just saying I need to accept my destiny and do the work...."

"That's good," Anna says. "It does take sacrifice to meet your destiny. And it's really important to imagine your creative pursuits as the sort of...like, healing process that you come to after you face your fears and demons and stuff."

"Right," I say.

"Maybe not *after* we face our fears," she adds. "I think it is the process by which we fight our demons."

"Right," I say again. Writing has helped me work through my anger, anxiety, insecurity. All the things I am still able to overcome.

I've long seen it as my duty to overcome what our mother couldn't. Her anger at the world and herself, which she passed on to me, and I struggle to keep in check every day. Then there's the cancer. I've been tested and I don't have the BRCA gene that can cause breast cancer, but it's possible our mother's was caused by a different gene. One way to tell, the doctor said, is to have Anna tested, too. If she is BRCA-positive, that would mean that while I'm safe, she's not. I don't know what I would do if I knew that.

"You should come visit me soon," I say. She was ambivalent about New York at first, but likes it more now that she has lived in a city. My friends all adore her. Even the ones who hate hippies can't help but find her charming.

"I've never met two sisters so different," my friend Max said when he first met Anna.

"I don't know," said my friend Meg. "I think you guys are two sides of the same coin."

Later that same night, I proved Meg's point when I took off my pinching shoes and walked barefoot along Lafayette Street.

"Maybe I will come visit," Anna says. "Oh! Guess what? That cat, Creamy, followed me home again today."

"Do you remember when we used to pretend we had a cat named Toasty?" I say.

"No, but I remember pretending to be Olympic gymnasts with a pet fish named Friendly."

"Oh yeah," I say. "We would scrape off flakes of crayon and pretend they were fish food."

She laughs, the same unusually deep laugh she's had since she was little. "Man, we were awesome."

"I was just thinking about the time I got chocolate syrup in your hair," I say to her. "Remember how I ended up washing it out in the kitchen sink—"

"In the *kitchen sink*?"

With Anna in 2015.
My little sister is now six inches taller than I am.

"—And then it got too cold and you screamed and I got in trouble?" I laugh. "But I tried."

"You did. You really did. You were always making me put on hand sanitizer." She laughs again. "You know, for a sister, you were a pretty good mom."

I smile. It's two in the morning, and I don't believe in blasphemy.

patterns

THERE'S A NIGHTMARE I had as a young child, the first one I can remember having. My mother was driving along a long stretch of highway, with me in the front seat. We passed a billboard, and on it was a ventriloquist's dummy, grinning eerily. As we drove on there was another billboard, and the dummy was bigger this time, even more full of menace. Another billboard, and at any moment, I just knew he would walk off the poster and into real life. I felt small and helpless and I knew only my mother could protect me. She seemed far away as I turned to her and said, "Mama, it's my worries again."

That's when I woke up. It wasn't an especially scary dream—a subconscious mash-up of *The Twilight Zone*, *Goosebumps*, and *The Simpsons*—but it has stayed with me, not because of the creepy image but because of what I said: "It's my worries *again*."

* * *

In most of my early childhood memories, I'm afraid. But it doesn't make sense. Nothing particularly traumatic happened that would explain how I became that way. There were earthquakes, but I knew how to stand in doorways and hide under tables. There were money woes, but while I saw my parents concerned about their finances, I never saw them panicked. I always had food and shelter, I always knew my family loved me. And yet I always felt as if something terrible was going to happen.

My mother was the only one who seemed to know how to ease the fear, the only one I believed when she said, "It's going to be okay."

"Just because Madeline got appendicitis doesn't mean you will," she told me.

"Tornadoes happen in other parts of the country, not in California."

"It's called the Devil's Punchbowl, but it's a place to go hiking. I don't care what the boys told you. We're Jewish, we don't even believe in the devil."

The only thing worse than being afraid of what might happen to me was being afraid of what *I* might do, even accidentally. My mother had one of her frequent meetings at the elementary school one day when I was four, and she left me outside on the grass field to play with her best friend's daughters, Laura and her older sister Kimberly. Laura and I spent an hour digging a small hole in the grass, but when I took a step back and looked at it, I started to cry.

"What's wrong?" asked Laura.

"What if someone steps in it and falls?" I said. "What if they get hurt?"

"They're going to see it and walk around it," said Kimberly.

"But what if they can't? What if they're *blind*?" I couldn't be consoled. Something bad could happen and it would be all my fault. My mind was stuck on fast-forward, always imagining the future as a worst-case scenario.

Thoughts would pop into my head sometimes, and I didn't understand why. They were bad thoughts, about people getting hurt or being embarrassed. After a Fourth of July celebration where a local actor had dressed up and walked around on stilts, a startling image of him popped into my head while we were walking home. My mother and grandmother didn't understand why I was crying, and were even more baffled after I explained it.

"You're thinking about Uncle Sam in his *underwear*?"

It was as confusing and exhausting for everyone else as it was for me.

"Mara's scared again," one of my brothers would say sighing, after I started crying at an *ALF* rerun or the "Black Hole Sun" music video, and I would feel ashamed. No one else in my family worried, at least not the way I did.

"Your brothers are afraid of things, too," my mother said. "Or at least they were when they were your age."

"Like what?"

"Danny used to be terrified of nuclear bombs." But Danny had been a small child at the tail end of the Cold War, so that wasn't entirely irrational.

My mother herself was not a worrier. She could be very tender with us, but when she wasn't in the mood to be gentle, she was angry. It seemed to be her only other mode. Every day she would find a reason to fly into a rage, then, within minutes, return back to neutral. The rages were never about anything serious.

"This is the stupidest song ever," she announced to no one and everyone as the Beatles' "You Like Me Too Much" came on the radio. "It's their worst song! Listen to it! Listen to how stupid it is! ''Cause you like me too much, and I like you'? That doesn't make any goddamn sense! That's not English! That's bullshit! This, from the greatest band of the twentieth century? Oh, oh, and the bridge—'I-I-I really do-o-o . . .'" She sang along and laughed out loud. "It's just so goddamn stupid!"

But as the song went on, her face softened, and she tilted her head, as if listening closer.

"It's not that bad," she said a moment later, not seeming to realize the sea change that had just taken place. She whistled along with a few bars, and shrugged. "It's a cute song."

None of us questioned her moods. Her unpredictability was predictable.

My mother found strength in anger. All her life, she had to be strong. Her parents had been in and out of hospitals most of their lives—my grandfather for diabetes and bipolar disorder, and my grandmother for chronic malingering—and she had been expected to care for her three younger siblings. The times she wasn't babysitting, she was studying, managing to secure a scholarship at Northwestern University. She valued nothing more than being tough and smart, and she was determined that her children would be, too. When I was three, she wrote "MARA: Tiny But Tough!" in fabric paint on a sweatshirt for me. I have been trying to live up to it my entire life.

I realized pretty early on that I wasn't, in fact, tough, but at least I could try to be smart. My first day of kindergarten, I brought home a cartoon Mickey Mouse standing next to a giant number one. I was just supposed to color him in, but that was too easy. He looked so proud, so presentational, I couldn't leave it at that.

"Mom," I said, "can you write him saying 'Presenting the Number One?'" She smiled, and did. She had the creative kid.

I was pleased with my position as the class overachiever, but had to relinquish it after I was given an impossible assignment: printing my name over and over again. Every time I tried, the letters were all a little too big, or too small, or too uneven. After I ripped the paper from erasing too much, my exhausted six-months-pregnant mother had had enough.

"You *know* how to do this!" she kept screaming. "You know how to spell it! You know how to print! Just write your goddamn name!"

"But it's not good enough!" I would scream back.

My brothers had a reputation for being smart. I was developing a slightly different reputation. My first-grade teacher, Mrs. Witt, paused before calling on me when I raised my hand during a lesson on earthquake preparedness.

"Is this another one of your 'what if' stories?" she asked, and I lowered my hand.

She knew I was a worrier, and she knew how hard I was on myself. The first time I got an answer wrong on a spelling test, I started to cry, and she pulled me aside.

"You know," she said, gently, "it's okay to make a mistake." I nodded until the encounter was over, then shook my head. I knew it wasn't.

It was one of my studio teachers who first gave my tendencies a name. Richard Wicklund was a well-traveled, intelligent man with years of experience teaching child actors on set (he had been the studio teacher for *The Goonies*) and an endless supply of funny stories. He was first assigned to me on the set of *Miracle*, but we ended up requesting him for every subsequent film. Richard understood how I learned best: the two of us would make up stories, hold debates, go on field trips to botanical gardens and science museums. He noticed how saying my lines aloud helped me learn them, so he taught me the multiplication tables by having me repeat them out loud.

I loved Richard, but things didn't always go smoothly. I would get angry when I couldn't get something right away, and he would have to talk me down. That usually made me angrier.

"You don't need to write so hard," he said once, noticing I already had a writer's callus on my middle finger at age seven.

"But—" I started to say.

"I know," he said. "You're a perfectionist." It didn't sound like a compliment.

There is no worse career for a perfectionist than filmmaking. When you're making a movie, nothing is more important than getting the shot right, preferably the first time, because time is money. It's not about learning or growing. It's not first grade and it's not okay to make a mistake.

I tried my best to get things right. When I was six, shortly before I filmed *Miracle*, I was cast in a made-for-TV movie that would eventually be titled *A Time to Heal*. Nicollette Sheridan was playing a woman who had a stroke after having a baby and had to relearn how to live her life. I was playing her daughter. One of the last scenes of the movie was us playing in the backyard after she had recovered, and her kicking a soccer ball into the goal. When she did, I was supposed to yell, "You made it, Mom, you made it!" and run up to her and Gary Cole for a big family hug.

On the first take, though, she missed the goal completely. I stood frozen, looking at Nicollette, not sure what to do.

"Cut!" the director yelled, and he came up to me. "Mara, next time, no matter what happens, just go ahead and say the line, okay? Even if she doesn't make the goal, we can just fix it later. Okay?"

"Okay," I promised. "No matter what."

I prepared myself as he called "Roll" again. This time, Nicollette kicked the soccer ball and it looked like it was going to make it, until at the last second it hit the goalpost. It bounced back, came flying back at us, and hit me full-on in the chest. It knocked the wind out of me, and I staggered back, trying to keep myself from falling over. I looked to Nicollette and Gary, who seemed horrified. What was I supposed to do?

"No matter what . . ." he'd said.

"You made it, Mom! You made it!" I screamed as loudly as I could, then ran over to Nicollette and Gary, my chest still stinging. As soon as the director called "Cut," the crew burst into laughter and applause, and I burst into tears.

My mother walked over, smiling gently, and I threw my arms around her.

"They're laughing at me!" I blubbered.

"No, they're clapping because you were being so professional," she said.

"I was *trying* to be," I said, still sobbing.

It felt like a job well done, but when I actually watched *A*

Time to Heal, I was appalled. In my most dramatic scene, they had chosen the one take where I broke and cracked a smile. I was angry with them, but I was angrier with myself. From then on, I never wanted to watch myself act onscreen. It was too painful. I was never good enough.

With my mother's cancer diagnosis, *Matilda*, my next film after *Miracle*, was a welcome distraction. Being on the set felt safe and comfortable. One morning when I was filming, I woke up and I just knew it would be a good day.

And it was. I got my takes done right the first time, craft service had Fudgsicles (*so* much better than the lemon Popsicles I usually had to settle for because the other flavors would make my tongue a funny color and thus ruin continuity), I had plenty of downtime to play with Kiami, Jacqueline, and all the other kids, and my mother had promised we could all go to the playground after work.

Lucy Dahl, Roald Dahl's daughter, was sitting nearby at lunch. She had kids, she'd listen to me. I waited for her to stop talking to the grown-ups at her table and turn to me.

"Guess what?" I said when she did. "I'm psychotic!"

She looked surprised. "Why do you think that?"

"Because I knew today was going to be a great day, and it *was* a great day!"

Lucy smiled. "You're not psychotic, Mara," she said, and my heart sank. "*Psychotic* means someone who's not connected to reality. I think you mean you're *psychic*, like you can predict the future."

"Oh," I said. "Yeah, that's what I am. Psychic!"

I spent the rest of the shoot predicting things.

"Kira, I predict you will get taller this year." Kira Spencer Hesser, who was playing Hortensia, was in sixth grade, and she was taller than all of us. Her mother was tall, too, so it was a safe bet.

"What do you think I'm going to be good at this school year?" Kiami asked me.

"Hmm . . . math and spelling," I said.

"I *am* good at math and spelling!" she said, and I smiled knowingly.

"Do me next," said Anthony, one of the older extra kids. "What sport will I play?"

"I bet you're good at basketball," I said.

"I'm not good at basketball, I'm good at football!"

"Maybe you'll be better in the future," I said.

It seemed fun while we were filming, but back in real life—where my mother was still sick, and I was afraid of the future, afraid of myself and what was in my mind—I realized that if I could predict good things, maybe I could predict bad things, too. Earthquakes I couldn't hide under the table from, getting kidnapped, something terrible happening to someone I loved . . .

"You're not psychic," my mother said. "That's magical thinking." It sounded like a fun way to describe something that was becoming increasingly terrifying. After *Matilda*, it was as if the background noise in my head had suddenly been turned up, and it was getting harder to control my thoughts.

I was suddenly very conscious of germs. They hadn't bothered me before, but now—perhaps in some way related to the fact that my mother had cancer complications the month we finished filming *Matilda*—they seemed to be everywhere. I never wanted to load the dishwasher, because it meant touching germy dishes. The boys at school were walking contamination: they burped the alphabet and made disgusting jokes and didn't even seem to wash their hands after using the bathroom. Girls could be gross, too: I saw my cousin picking her nose, and she called me "paranoid" when I told her to wash her hands before and after playing with my hamster. You couldn't trust anyone to be clean enough.

Every day after school, I would immediately go into the bathroom and wash my hands. The graphite dust and blacktop turned the water a murky color, and I would feel a sense of relief and satisfaction. More and more, though, I was starting to notice that even when they didn't look dirty, they *felt* dirty. I'd return to the sink for another round with Softsoap.

My hands became perpetually chapped. No one in my family seemed especially concerned at first, as I'd always had dry, sensitive skin. My mother applied lotions, and as they got even more red and raw, she switched to ointments and mineral oils. Nothing seemed to work: I was washing her concoctions off before they had a chance to sink in.

Things got worse the day a friend who was over forgot to put my hamster away. Even after we found her, I cried all night. Was she still safe? Still there? I put a safety pin on one door of her cage and tied a ribbon on the other to secure them, but even that didn't alleviate my concerns. Every hour I would get out of bed and check to see if Eleanor was still in her cage. For weeks, I didn't sleep through the night, and every time I thought of her getting out I would have the same body-shaking, short-of-breath, mind-racing panic I'd had that first night. I was afraid of being afraid, and I didn't want to lose Eleanor. I didn't want to lose anything.

"For God's sake!" my mother yelled when I woke her up for the third time in one night. "Eleanor got out because Fiona *took* her out! She's fine! Go back to sleep!"

"But I'm scared, Mom," I wailed. I knew she was ill and needed rest, but I couldn't help it. I needed her.

"Jesus, Mara." She sighed. "Do we have to put you in a goddamn straitjacket? You're being insane!"

It hurt more because I believed it was true: I thought I was losing my mind. I would walk down the hall and suddenly think, *You can't walk that way.* If I did, something terrible would happen. I didn't tell anyone about these thoughts. To my eight-year-old mind, having thoughts like these meant I was hearing voices in my head, which meant I was schizophrenic, which meant I was crazy, which meant I would soon be locked up in a padded cell away from the rest of the world.

Every time I walked through the doorway from the family room to the front room, I had to duck under the pencil mark someone had made two and a half feet off the floor. There was an invisible line extending from it to the other side, and I felt like it would cut me in half. The space between an open door and the threshold wasn't safe, either, and when no one was looking, I would jump over it.

My mother caught me one day as I came into her room.

"I've seen you doing this," she said, curled up in bed, looking serious. "What is it? Is there something on the floor?"

"I . . ." I couldn't lie to my mother. It wasn't possible. "I . . . feel like I have to jump over that little space."

There was a long silence, and then she laughed. It was the last month she was alive, and whether she sensed that or not, she knew she had to pick her battles. Maybe she was just too sick and tired to fight it anymore. Maybe she was hoping I would laugh, too. And I did: It was silly. I knew it didn't matter, but I still believed it. I didn't have a choice. It was the same way that, no matter how often she had told me we didn't believe in Hell, I was still afraid of going there. Sometimes, when the panic overtook me, I wondered if I was already there.

As my old fears faded, new ones took their place. After my mother died, I would look at the little things she had placed on my desk, and I knew I couldn't move them. She had put them there for a reason. I couldn't get rid of anything she might have touched. Stepping over the doorway the right way was suddenly no longer a problem, but instead, I needed to check under the bathroom sink to make sure no one had installed a camera to spy on me. I didn't know why anyone would do that, and I knew I wouldn't find one, but I still had to check.

The world seemed to operate on a kind of internal logic, a system of Bad Luck and Good Luck, and I had to be careful with it. I believed every superstition I'd ever heard. If I kept saying that one *Simpsons* quote to myself, I would get an A on my history test, like I had that one time. If I hummed the score from *The Wizard of Oz*, I would have a bad day. (Maybe the Cowardly Lion's "I even scare myself sometimes!" hit too close to home.) What was Good Luck one day could be Bad Luck another day. Five was a bad number, but after I turned nine, eight became a bad number, too. There were patterns everywhere, everything was connected, but I didn't understand how.

The worst part about my fears was how isolated I felt. When I felt bad, I knew no one would understand. If I was feeling better, I didn't want to see anyone who had been around when I was doing worse. They might ask how I was and send me into a spiral, just by reminding me of how I'd been feeling before.

A few months before *Matilda* came out, Embeth and I met at a sound studio to rerecord some of our dialogue. Embeth and I had bonded during *Matilda*, and she felt like an older sister to me.

I loved Embeth, but I had also seen her the week I had my first panic attack. Seeing her again could be Bad Luck. She said, "How are you?" and I just shrugged and looked away.

"I brought you something," she said, smiling, and drew a heart in the air. She had invited me over to her house for tea when we first started filming, and we had split a giant heart-shaped cookie sandwich with rich chocolate fudge in the middle. It was the most decadent thing I could imagine, and from then on she would bring one to the set for me on special occasions. She must have brought one for me.

"Oh, okay, thanks," I mumbled, and asked Danny DeVito if I could go to the bathroom. I tried not to look at her for the rest of the time we were recording. What else could I do?

My father came to my door that night as I was doing my homework.

"Embeth called," my father said, and my heart sank. "She asked if you were okay. She said you seemed to be avoiding her."

"Oh," I said, and didn't say anything more. I was learning that it was hard to lie to my father, too.

"Why were you so rude to her?"

"I . . . I don't know," I said. "I didn't want to be."

"Go call her back and apologize."

Embeth accepted my apology readily, but I still felt terrible. I couldn't explain why I had acted that way, not really. I hated my fears and I hated myself. As I hung up the phone, I started to cry. I walked into the kitchen, expecting to be alone, but my father was sitting there.

"Why are you crying?"

I thought of all the times I had woken up from a nightmare and called for my mother. I thought of the first time my father had opened the door instead, and how confused I had felt. But then I thought about the nights those first few weeks after her death, when he had stayed by my side until I fell asleep.

A Mama's Girl in her daddy's arms.

"Dad, what do I do when I get scared?"

"You learn to control it." He took a sip from his stein, which, as always, was filled to the brim with English breakfast tea rather than beer.

"How do I do that?" I said.

"The same way you control your own two hands."

". . . What?"

He was afraid of things when he was my age, too, he told me, but he had learned to control it. When they were things he was afraid to do, he made himself do them. When they were abstract ideas, he told himself not to dwell on what wasn't rational and what was out of his control.

It was good advice, but not for someone like me. I didn't have any control over what I thought or did. My father didn't know what happened in my mind, and I couldn't ever tell him. He wouldn't be able to understand. He wouldn't love me anymore if he knew. He would leave.

By the time I was eleven years old, I was sure there was no way I was ever going to be better. Nothing seemed to help. My mother had gotten into yoga and meditation when she was sick, and, like any other L.A. kid, I had tried it, too. Breathing and focusing could help relieve my anxiety, but every time I tried it on my own, I always got too distracted by my own thoughts. Guidance counselors at school would ask me about my mother, but I didn't know what to say. I wasn't ready to talk about her. The grown-ups around me talked about my "anxiety," but they never said "disorder." Nobody seemed to want to acknowledge there was something wrong with me. It was just my age, they said, or a stage of grief, but one that would pass. I would grow out of it.

Many kids go through a period of intense worrying in their preteen years, as they learn what's true about the world and what's not. But I didn't know any kids who worried like I did. My mind didn't even seem to work the same way as theirs. My friends would talk about getting songs stuck in their heads, and I knew what they meant; I had "It's Raining Men" stuck in my head for most of my preteen years. It wasn't just songs in mine, though: words, phrases, names, and quotes all seemed to get stuck, too. It was Captain McCallister from *The Simpsons* yelling "Jonathan Livingston Seagull!" or just the name "Janine" repeated over and over until I wasn't sure it was a name anymore. They didn't bother me so much, just stuck around like background noise that would come to my attention now and then, like when you suddenly notice a clock ticking.

But the bad thoughts also stuck around, and they were popping up more and more as I got older. Out of nowhere I would think of something horrific, and it would be so intense and detailed, so much scarier than the horror movies I was too scared to watch, it would leave me shaking. These waking nightmares always seemed to be about the people I loved most, the ones I most wanted to protect: my friends, my family, my pets, even God. I didn't want to hurt people, and I didn't enjoy these thoughts, but I didn't know why they would even be in my mind. Either I was a horrible person or I was a crazy person. Either way, I had to hide it.

Weeks would pass where I felt normal, or at least as normal as I ever was, with my worries at a livable level. My hands would be cracked but not bleeding. I would tap out syllables of songs or quotes on my fingers repeatedly, until the last one landed on my pinkie, but it wouldn't make me physically uncomfortable if I couldn't. I wouldn't have to use an entire bottle of Purell hand sanitizer in a single evening just to feel "clean." Then something would change. It could be triggered by something big—Eleanor dying, somehow managing to fail my art/music/PE class—but often it didn't matter what was happening; any day could become a stressful day. Sometimes I would just think about how long it had been since I had those panicky feelings, and it would start up again. The first day would be awful, and I would refuse to eat, shower three or four times a day, and cry myself to sleep. The second day I would feel better, and by the third day it would be gone. I would feel relieved, but only temporarily—I knew it was bound to happen again.

In sixth grade I spent a lot of time alone, racked with panic, crying in bathroom stalls. By seventh grade, however, I had a solid group of friends, who had also been given the both distinguished and damning title of Gifted and Talented, and were fine with being weird. Some were also child actors, some would grow up to be gay, some would grow up to be comedians. If I needed to escape the secret bloodbath in my brain, I could always talk to one of them. "You look at things in the coolest ways," one of them would say, and I would shrug: it was easy for me to be philosophical when *everything* was in question. We would role-play in private chat rooms, and they would tell me to pretend to be the germ-phobic Lysol Queen again. We joked about "the little voices in our heads" that made us do things. They were quirky, and they accepted my quirks.

Would they, though, if they knew how weird I really was? If they knew I *did* have little voices, little thoughts in my own head that made me jump over cracks in the floor and imagine hurting my own family? If they knew I sometimes felt so overwhelmed with fear and misery that I thought about killing myself? I doubted it. There was no one I could completely trust, and I definitely couldn't trust myself. My friends and I could laugh at school and joke around on the phone, but when I hung up, I was alone.

* * *

By this time, I had heard the term "obsessive-compulsive." I figured it was another way of saying "perfectionist"; it was a personality trait, and one I probably had. Being a brunette meant I had brown hair, being outgoing meant I liked to meet and talk to people, and being obsessive-compulsive meant I washed my hands a lot. I'd been called worse.

"Do you want some hand sanitizer?" I said to the one girl at camp who seemed as dirt averse as me. "I'm obsessive-compulsive like that." It was a phrase I'd decided to apply to myself before anyone else could.

Two months in Toronto changed everything. Richard, my studio teacher on *Miracle*, couldn't make it up to Canada to work with me during *Thomas*, so Lisa Jakub, my *Doubtfire* costar, who had been doing movies in Canada since she was four, recommended a woman named Laurie. Laurie and I bonded quickly. She was warm and friendly, open-minded and upbeat, the living embodiment of every positive Canadian stereotype.

I hadn't been a good student for years. I got distracted by my own thoughts, and gave up too readily. Being smart felt like all I had, and if I couldn't get something right the first time, everyone would know I wasn't. If I couldn't do it perfectly, I didn't see the point of doing it at all.

But I was a good student with Laurie. She, like Richard, quickly figured out how I learned. The first day of classes, I asked her a question about the history of the Crusades, and we ended up spending two hours talking about our issues with organized religion. The second day, I told her how much I hated having to read *A*

Day No Pigs Would Die, and we ended up spending two hours talking about historical romance and romanticizing history and how I thought *Titanic* was totally overrated.

She listened to me, and I felt comfortable talking to her. I sensed I could tell her anything, and she wouldn't judge. The third day, I went out on a limb.

"I'm weird," I said.

"It's all right to be a little weird," she said. "There's a saying I like: 'I am a raisin in the rice pudding of life.'"

I laughed, but the uneasiness in my chest was still there. I needed someone to know what I had been going through.

"No, but I'm *really* weird," I said. "I'm a perfectionist. I worry about everything all the time—about stuff nobody else ever worries about. I'm scared of everything. And I'm totally obsessive-compulsive."

At that, Laurie put out her hand, inviting me to shake it. "Welcome to the club. I am, too."

She was, too? Someone else knew! Someone else carried around hand sanitizer and opened bathroom doors with paper towels, too! I had so many questions.

"How do you deal with it? Do people ever think you're crazy? Do you worry about things a lot, too? Like . . . bad things happening to your family and dogs and stuff?"

"I do worry," she said. "I think everyone does, but some of us just worry more. And I think what's most important is thinking about what you can control."

There was that word again. I didn't know if I would ever be able to control it, but I felt heartened. I was allowed to be worried, and somehow, that alone made me feel a little less worried.

* * *

Thomas quickly became almost as much fun to make as *Matilda*. Laurie; my nanny, Lucy; and I would go to the mall and write it off as "Physical Education." We would get hot chocolate at Second Cup and roll our eyes at whatever Alec Baldwin had done on set that day, then binge-watch *Absolutely Fabulous*. Laurie took us ice skating ("This is Canada, honey," she said when I asked why there weren't any walls in the rink), and I got to see snow falling for the first time. We all read Harry Potter and *To Kill a Mockingbird*. Sometimes we would let Michael Rodgers, whom I had a big crush on, tag along with us on our field trips, but mostly it was a girls' club. I hadn't felt that consistently happy in years.

Hanging with some llamas on a crew member's farm with Laurie. This is about the only positive male attention I got in middle school.

But I couldn't completely distract myself. At night, the anxiety would catch up with me. The attacks seemed to come on days I hadn't slept very much, so I had become obsessed with getting enough sleep. The prospect of getting less than seven hours was enough to send me into a panic. There is a twelve-hour turnaround between wrap and the next day's call time for child actors, but with travel time, homework, and calling my friends and family back home, I was often cutting it close. I would stare at the clock and cry as the numbers got bigger and then smaller, feeling helpless. Worst-case scenario, I thought, I could always cry myself to sleep.

One of those nights, Lucy heard me crying and came into my room.

"Just focus on your breathing," she said in her gentle British accent.

"It's going to be so bad if I don't sleep enough," I said.

"That's not happening now. You're safe now. Just think of your breathing, think of calm blue waters." I never understood how she could be so calm and steady. She was never anything less than positive. I wished I could be more like her, or even Laurie, who was anxious but had it under control.

There were many more nights like that.

"It won't work," I told her once, after she had sat with me for what seemed like an hour. "Nothing's going to work. No matter how much sleep I get, I'm always tired."

Lucy was quiet for a long time, and then she said, "I think that's depression, darling."

It was the first time an adult had ever suggested something might be wrong with me. Instead of feeling upset, I felt grateful. I reached out for Lucy and hugged her. If I did have depression, if I could be sure that was it, if I could just identify the patterns, maybe I could get better.

For the first week home after *Thomas*, I was miserable. I had gotten so used to Lucy and Laurie being there for me, listening to me, and I felt lost without them. They might as well have been gone forever. I should have felt better by the third day, like always, but I didn't. The panic was back. I couldn't eat. I couldn't sleep. I couldn't do anything but cry.

My father sat with me as I lay curled up in a ball, sobbing into a pillow.

"I'll bet it was probably really nice to spend time with such nice women, wasn't it?"

"It was," I said. Another wave of anxiety rocked through me, and I sobbed harder.

"How about we go up to the mountains tonight?" he said. "There's a meteor shower. We can sit back and watch it. Bring some lawn chairs and hot chocolate."

"Okay," I said into the pillow. He could be so kind. It was too much. Something could happen and I could lose him.

He stroked my hair and stood up, pausing when he got to the door.

"You can still talk to them, you know."

It was a good idea. Lucy and I started e-mailing, and I could call Laurie as long as it wasn't too late. They always seemed happy to hear from me. "Tell me how you're doing," they would ask, and I would tell them the truth, all the things I never told my father.

"What's good in your life?" Laurie asked one night. "Are you reading anything interesting?"

"Not really," I said. All I wanted to read was Harry Potter and *To Kill a Mockingbird*, like I had in Toronto, over and over again.

"Get some new books," Laurie suggested. "That will help. Reading always helps."

"I got a book brochure in class," I said. "I'll order some new books."

On the front page of the brochure was a book called *Kissing Doorknobs*. The description said it was about a preteen girl who was always scared and did strange things no one seemed to understand. She had obsessive-compulsive disorder.

Disorder. What did that mean? Obsessive-compulsive meant perfectionistic. It didn't also mean being superstitious and nervous and worried all the time, did it? That's what the description seemed to suggest, but I couldn't believe it. Was it possible that all my weirdnesses connected? I had to read it. I'd already spent last week's allowance on the first two Everworld books and *Bloomability*, but I decided to forgo my usual trip to Walgreens to buy peanut butter cups and use this week's allowance on another book instead.

It arrived two weeks later, a black cover with colorful drawings of doorknobs, and the author's name, Terry Spencer Hesser, stamped on the front. The name seemed familiar, but I soon forgot about that when I started reading. The first few pages were uncanny. The main character, whose name was Tara, got words and thoughts stuck in her head, just like I did. She tapped out syllables, just like I did. She was afraid to step on lines on the floor or the pavement, just like I was. She had "impure," scary thoughts, and attacks where the anxiety took over her whole body. Her friends and family didn't understand, and she was scared to tell them.

"Oh my God," I said out loud when I finished the first chapter.

My friend Melissa, who was sitting next to me during silent reading, put down *Watership Down* and whispered, "What is it?"

"This book is the story of my life."

I read it all afternoon, even risking motion sickness by reading it in the car on the way home from school. If Tara's fears and "quirks" were familiar, her parents' reactions were even more so. Her mother got angry at her when she counted or prayed. She yelled, like my mother had, or threatened to hit her, or sent her to her room. She thought she could punish her daughter's fears away.

Tara got angry herself, yelling at her friends when they got in the way of her counting cracks in the sidewalk. I thought of all the times I had been angry. The time I'd screamed at my little sister, Anna, not to hold my hand after we rode the escalator in the mall together, because she had touched the handrail and it was dirty. The time a wave of fear had overtaken me while we were in PE, and I had thrown down my racquet and yelled, "JUST SERVE THE GODDAMN BALL!" so loudly the seagulls on the gym roof went flying away. Being angry was easier than being scared.

I never thought my mother was afraid, but she must have been. She just hid it behind anger. She had seen her father struggle with bipolar disorder, and resented the personality disorder that made her mother behave like a perpetual victim, unable to take care of herself. She must have been scared I would suffer like they had.

Tara's father was the opposite of her mother, quiet and stoic, like my father. When he broke down at the end because Tara couldn't leave the house without kissing the doorknob thirty-seven times, I started to cry, too.

And then her father's friend said he knew what it was: Tara had obsessive-compulsive disorder. It was why she was anxious and why she did strange things. It was because of genetics and brain chemistry, and it wasn't her fault. She could be helped. Tara went to therapy, learned to face her fears, and even met a cute guy who washed his hands too much, too. The last line of the book was "And we weren't alone." I was still sobbing, but now it was with relief.

"Are you okay?" both my father and Joel asked at dinner. My eyes were red and I wasn't eating.

"I have a headache," I said, which was true.

"Do you need medicine?" said Anna, but I shook my head. The kind of headache that comes from crying too much can't be helped by Advil.

It was eight o'clock, eleven Toronto time, but I needed to call Laurie.

"I think I know what's wrong with me," I told her. "I think I have obsessive-compulsive disorder. Real OCD. It's not just me washing my hands, it's all my fears and my scary thoughts and everything. It's all connected." A pattern, I thought, tracing one in the carpet.

"That may be what it is," she said.

"What do I do now, though?" I said, and the tears came back to my eyes. "Am I ever going to get better?"

"Here's what you can do," she said. "Take the book to your father—"

"No, I can't do that!" I said. "He'll be too upset! He'll get worried! I don't want to worry him."

"All right, then," she said, after a beat. "Take it to your guidance counselors. They will be able to talk to your father, and find someone who can help you."

The next day I went to the counseling office during lunch hours, clutching my dog-eared copy of *Kissing Doorknobs*. They agreed that there did seem to be something very familiar about it. There were intermediate steps, they explained. *Diagnostic Manuals* to consult and papers to sign, and a list of my own symptoms to make. They would give me a referral, but I would have to tell my father myself.

I went to him after dinner, when he was alone at the kitchen table with his stein of tea and a book about spy planes.

"Um, Dad?"

His eyes were bleary. He had been working the early shift at the KTLA morning news again, going to work in Hollywood at four-thirty in the morning. I put *Kissing Doorknobs* and the psychologist's card down on the table, and looked at the linoleum floor.

"Um . . . you remember when I was crying yesterday before dinner? It was because of this book. Not because it made me upset, but because . . . because I think the girl in this book has the same problem I do. And I think I can get help for it, and I really want to."

My father closed his eyes and pinched the top of his nose, like he did when he had a headache. He was silent.

"How about we take a trip over spring break?" he said finally. "We can go to Nevada, go to the lakes, the mountains. Maybe stop by some buffets and arcades in Vegas or Reno."

"Um, okay," I said. Not the response I had hoped for.

He stood up and walked out of the kitchen, leaving *Kissing*

Doorknobs and the card on the table. I would have to sneak it into his suitcase.

He brought it back to me on the last day of our trip. Anna had fallen asleep in the motel bed next to me. I was lying in bed reading *Bloomability* and fantasizing about going away to boarding school someday when my father came into the room carrying *Kissing Doorknobs*. He set it down on the nightstand, and before he could make a move to tuck me in, like he did every night, I sat up.

"Did you read it?"

He crouched down and gave me a hug.

"You don't need to worry about this, honey. You're going to grow out of it. You'll be okay. You're not insane—"

"I know I'm not *insane*, Dad," I said, and my voice was shaking. "I'm obsessive-compulsive. It's different. But it's a disorder. I want to get help for it."

He stood up and walked to the window. Immediately, I felt sorry. Not sorry for telling him the truth, but sorry he had to hear it.

We drove home the next morning. Anna and I made up stories and sang along to the radio, but my father was silent. He went into his room when we got home. Two days later, I was sitting in the front room, looking out the window, when he came up to me.

"I called that doctor," he said. "We talked for a while about OCD. She says the kids who have it . . . well, it really wears on them."

"It does," I said.

"I made an appointment for next Friday," he said. "After school."

"Thank you," I said.

That same week I found a book called *Everything in Its Place* on our kitchen table. It was written by Marc Summers, who had worked as a host for Nickelodeon and had OCD.

"Is this for me?" I asked my father when he came in.

"Yeah, take a look at it," he said. "I met Marc Summers once at work. He was a good guy. I thought it might interest you."

I stood up and wrapped my arms around my father.

"I love you, Dad."

"I love you, too. I love you to pieces."

My official diagnosis was made in about five minutes. Dr. Graham sat with me and my copy of *Kissing Doorknobs*, and listened as I told her everything that had made life miserable for the past four years.

Then she asked if she could call in my father. He sat across from us and nodded solemnly as she explained that I did have OCD. Before we left she gave him another card, one for a psychiatrist.

As we drove home, I felt lighter. Giving what I had a label meant it could be addressed. I was going to get better.

"Do you think I should tell anyone?" I said.

My father looked pensive. He must have been wondering who I meant by "anyone." My friends? My *fans*?

"I wouldn't," he said, "at least not yet."

But my need to confess was too strong. I had to tell someone. So I decided I would tell the people who already knew, more or less. I called Laurie.

"The doctor says I do have OCD."

"How do you feel about that?"

"Honestly?" I said. "Like, really relieved. I don't feel bad about it. I can't help it, so why should I feel bad about it, you know?"

"You shouldn't," she said.

"But my dad . . . well, I think he wants me to keep it a secret."

"I can understand that," she said. "If the media got hold of it—well, the media is terrible enough already. Look what they do to those poor girls with eating disorders."

"That's true," I said.

I did find a way to tell my brothers and my little sister.

"That sucks, and I'm sorry you have to deal with that. But really, Mara, in our family? That's not so bad," said Danny.

"Yeah," said Jon, and he started to laugh. "Honestly, with our genetic history, it's kind of impressive you're only neurotic."

My sobs turned into laughs. We went through the laundry list of diagnoses I could have had, all the possible disorders our ancestors could have given us. It could have been worse.

Dr. Rosenbaum didn't end up needing the checklists I'd filled out on the intake form. It was clear to him that I had "severe OCD," and some other things, too. "Anxiety attacks, a little bit of generalized anxiety, post-traumatic stress disorder, depression."

"It's not just OCD?" I said, a little bothered. It would have been nice if everything had fit neatly into one diagnosis.

"OCD has a lot of related disorders," he said. "The ones you have, and others. Tourette's syndrome, trichotillomania, stuff like that. Do you want to go on medication?"

"I want to do whatever helps," I said. "But if I have more than OCD . . . Are you sure I don't have anything else? Bipolar or schizophrenia? I think they may run in my family."

"You don't," he said. "Not now, anyway. It could be possible you might when you're older, but now you don't have symptoms."

"Okay, because sometimes I worry I hear voices."

"Well, are they inside your head or outside your head?"

"Inside," I said.

"If you can recognize that it's coming from your own mind, it isn't schizophrenia. It's probably just standard OCD intrusive thoughts. Worrying about having other disorders is a common OCD symptom itself, actually."

"Okay." I felt relieved, and I felt braver. "And even if I ever *do* have schizophrenia or bipolar disorder, or whatever, there are ways to treat it, right?"

"Right," he said, smiling gently.

When I came home from the psychiatrist, Jon asked how it had gone.

"Good," I said. "I mean, he says I have OCD, but also panic attacks and maybe some other stuff, but now that we know, we can make it better. He says it waxes and wanes. I think I'm going to go on Zoloft."

"Yeah, you know, I have a friend at Hopkins who has anxiety," said Jon. "It's rough on her, but she says it's better now that she's on medication."

A girl was open about her anxiety? I couldn't wait to get to college.

On the last day of seventh grade, over lunch at the mall's food court, I told my friends. They were concerned, but not horrified. They just wanted me to feel better. When I brought up *Kissing Doorknobs*, Sierra suggested a trip to the bookstore, so they could buy copies and understand it better.

I didn't tell many people, but those I did tell seemed to understand. My favorite teacher at my middle school, Mrs. Vollman, told me one of her best friends also had panic attacks. Anna's best friend's mother let me hang out in their garden and play with their cats when I felt anxious. I poured my heart out to the teacher who showed me around Idyllwild Arts Academy when I was fifteen, and she was remarkably unfazed.

"If you do come here," she said, "you will find so many other students who have also been through all that."

If I got in, I decided, I was going to be open about it. I would be on my own there, away from my family, and it would be my decision. If I didn't act like it was a big deal, maybe no one else would think it was a big deal.

And that was how it went. At Idyllwild, I found a way to work it into conversations as soon as I could. All the friends I made knew the truth about me. Bonnie, my adviser, knew it. Keith, the soft-spoken school psychologist, knew it. None of them judged me. None of them thought I was weird. Anxiety disorders, ADD, and depression were common, and some of the other students had come to Idyllwild right from rehab schools or hospitals. The girls in my hall and I would compare notes on therapies and medications, bonding with our own kind of gallows humor.

"Dude, the nighttime pill-delivery guy is super hot."

"So I went to the infirmary today because I had a panic attack, and they let me watch *Ferris Bueller's Day Off.*"

"Are you going to be okay? You can sleep in my room tonight if you need to."

For the first time, I knew I wasn't alone.

Some of my symptoms went away on their own as I got older. Some of them were kept in check with Zoloft. There was never

*Having my first snowball fight at age sixteen. Fast
Times at Idyllwild Arts Academy!*

one big relapse for me, but there were several little ones. Shortly
before I went to Idyllwild, I went through a period of severe
depression where I would compulsively pull out my hair, and
occasionally withdraw and feel like I was in a dream. The hair
pulling, or trichotillomania, stopped with a readjustment of
meds and the change of scenery, but I did still go into a dreamlike dissociative state when I was feeling overwhelmed. Once I
got to college and was in a program designed to open me up as a
performer and person, where I was required to focus and constantly evaluate myself, I found I couldn't dissociate anymore
and my panic attacks got worse. At that point, I had to learn how
to deal with my panic attacks on my own, by working with a new
therapist and using a book called the *Panic Attacks Workbook*. I

was finally strong enough to do what my father had suggested years before: tackle my fears, head-on.

It was one of my professors who gave me what has become my philosophy on anxiety.

"How do you think your show went?" my teacher Tomi asked me in a meeting after I finished a run of my one-woman show in my senior year. She had always given me good advice, like suggesting I bring some of my anger into my work and some of the kindness and vulnerability she saw in my writing into my life.

"In the end, I think it went pretty well," I said.

"How did you feel while you were working on it?"

"Kind of nervous," I said. "Actually, really nervous. I was a nervous wreck the whole time."

Tomi smiled and nodded. "That's fine. It's okay to be nervous."

"I always am," I said.

"What I would suggest is you own yourself as an anxious person."

It stuck in my head, but this time, for the right reasons. Own my anxieties and I wouldn't be letting them own me. It is one of the many bits of wisdom I wish I had when I was eight.

Here's what I've learned: If you're worried you have a psychosis, you probably don't, but even if you do, there's help for it. Fighting with anxiety makes it worse; instead, accept the anxiety, and it will become less scary. Take a moment to breathe and take stock of your surroundings. Remember what's real. Say, "This sucks, but it will pass." We aren't responsible for our thoughts, we are only responsible for what we do with them. Mental health care can and should be taken as seriously as physical health care.

A diagnosis is not a bad thing. Some of the most interesting people in the world have been through what you have. Above all, you are not alone.

There is still so much misinformation about OCD. When I was diagnosed, it was something sitcom characters had, a tendency or personality type. The Internet has made perception of it worse in some ways: OCD has become an adjective, something linkbait websites use to get people to look at funny pictures of a pencil out of line. If there's one thing I can do to combat the misinformation, it's to be open about my experience.

I still worry. I'll always worry. *I could do a whole show about all my anxieties*, I thought to myself on a stressful day in 2013. A few months later, I hosted the first installment of my oral storytelling show *What Are You Afraid Of?*, which is all about fears, anxieties, phobias—dealing with them, and laughing at them. Everyone's afraid of something, but talking about fear takes away its power.

I don't believe in patterns the way I once did. If something is a coincidence or seems to happen for a reason, I believe it's due to chance, or to the way our minds work, looking for patterns and shaping events into stories to help us make sense of everything.

But there's one very important coincidence I can't dismiss quite as easily.

Back in the days when I used to respond to questions on a fan page forum, one person included a few questions about *Matilda* that caught me off guard. Had Kiami and I really been friends, she asked, as many had before her. (The answer was yes.)

"How about you and Kira Spencer Hesser?"

She had more questions after that, but I stopped in my tracks.

Kira, who played Hortensia? Her last name was Spencer Hesser? My heart started beating fast, and faster.

I opened up the DVD of *Matilda* and skipped forward to the credits. There she was, Kira Spencer Hesser. Kira was from Chicago. Terry Spencer Hesser, the author of *Kissing Doorknobs*, was from Chicago. Kira's mother had been on set with her every day, and now I remembered: her name was Terry. I had met her five years before her book had changed my life.

Through social media, I found Kira. She was an actress and comedian in L.A., even funnier, cooler, and taller than I remembered. Feeling a little shy, I sent her a message.

"Mara! How are you, my sweet?" She was as friendly as ever. "How did my mom change your life?"

I wrote out the whole story of my OCD, stumbling on the book, and how it led me to find treatment. Kira wrote me back the next day. She had read my message and cried, then shared it with her mother, and the two of them had cried together.

"What a powerful thing it is, to put things like words and images out in the world and not know how they are received, and then to hear stories like yours all these many years later," wrote Kira, describing her mother's reaction.

It is, and it's why I keep going. It's why I will talk about OCD, about fear, about anxiety, to anyone who will hear it.

One day, I will have Kira and Terry on *What Are You Afraid Of?* Then, finally, the pattern will be complete.

i think i'm alone now

"CLEAN."

"Clean."

"Dirty."

"Sport."

I was hanging out with a bunch of child actors turned pubescent teenage actors after a charity event, and we were playing a game we'd made up ourselves, one we played after Kill/Marry/Screw got too tame.

The game was called Clean/Dirty/Sport. It involved going around a circle to each person—either just the people of our preferred gender or everyone, assuming some kind of hypothetical bisexuality—and saying how we would have sex with them, if we were to. "Clean" meant sweet and romantic, rose petals and candles, that kind of thing. "Dirty" meant "kinky," though what "kinky" meant, none of us really knew. We were all under fifteen, and none of us seemed to have actually had sex. At some point, someone had complained that "clean" seemed too boring and "kinky" seemed too scary, so we added another category, "sport."

"'Sport' means, like, quick and hot, you know?" said whoever suggested it. "Like, remember that monologue in *Fight Club* where he says it's like a sport? It's like that." And we all nodded and murmured and pretended we knew what "sport" meant, because it wasn't cool to admit you hadn't seen *Fight Club* (I had only seen the end, effectively ruining the rest of the movie for me). If we had, we would have known no such monologue existed.

On this particular day, my results had been mixed, but now it was a boy named Zack's turn to go around the circle. Like me, he was ethnically Jewish, but like every other teenager in California, he considered himself a Buddhist. He was an actor, too, though his name would be unrecognizable to anyone who didn't spend an inordinate amount of time watching Disney Channel Original Movies in the late nineties. He looked like the nerdy character in a Brat Pack movie.

He had been on the periphery for as long as I'd known him, since the night two years before when my costar from *Thomas*, Cody, had introduced us.

"You're Mara Wilson? Whoa, *the* Mara Wilson?" he had said when we first met. "Actually, I've never heard your name before. Who are you?" he added hilariously. "I'm Zack." He put out his hand, and I shook it.

We riffed off each other and he gave me his AOL Instant Messenger screen name. We talked a little online, I saw him at Kids with a Cause events, he came to my show choir's annual concert to see a mutual friend and gave me a hug after. I had always thought well of him, but never as anything more than a friend. But when Zack's eyes settled on me, something changed. It was as if I was seeing him clearly for the first time. Maybe it was the way he had played his guitar at our last event—I couldn't imagine anything sexier than musical talent—but as he sized me up, I wanted to do something, say something, make sure I would stand out.

"Clean," he said, and I leaped on an impulse.

"Huh," I said, looking him straight in the eye. "You must not know me very well."

"OHHHHH!" the rest of the table yelled, in unison. Zack said nothing, just sat wide-eyed, adorably shocked.

He was fifteen and had just broken up with his second "real" girlfriend. I was fourteen and had never had a boyfriend. I didn't know anything about sex, let alone "dirty" sex. Everyone knew that. I was a nice girl who talked big. But Zack's eyes were opened. He was seeing me in a new way, too, and I knew it.

"I always did find you incredibly sexy, Mara," he told me in an instant message a few months later.

We had just been talking about music videos, so I assumed he was joking. I was generally oblivious to any romantic overtures. Even the time Marco from chemistry class had gazed deep into my eyes and sung the Spanish love song "A Veces Quiero Llorar" to me, I didn't think anything of it.

"Maybe it's just the 'look at the little girl from *Mrs. Doubtfire* all grown up' thing," he added. That was a thing?

"You're funny, Zack," I typed.

"Yeah, but I'm not joking," he typed back. "I've had a shitty day. I'm always honest when I have a shitty day. You're sexy."

"Oh. Well . . . thank you."

"We should do something sometime," he said, and my heart started beating faster. It didn't seem to slow down until a few days later, when I realized he wasn't going to be the one to follow up. When I did call him, he seemed dismissive.

"Yeah, if you want to do something, or whatever, I think Lauren and I are going to go see *The Boner Identity* later today," he said.

"The—oh, you mean *The Bourne Identity*? Today?" I said. "That's kind of last minute. My parents are really strict, they need to know stuff in advance."

"All right, then, I'll see you another time, I guess."

He had pulled the oldest trick in the teenage boy book: paying attention to a girl, then ignoring her. And it had worked: I couldn't stop thinking about him. I always hoped he was online, hoped he would be at another Kids with a Cause event, hoped he would call me again and ask me out for real this time.

We never did meet up that day. In the months that followed, he left a few messages on my parents' answering machine. They were not impressed.

"That Zack guy," my stepmother said, shaking her head. "Every time he calls he's just like 'Hey, Mara, it's Zack. I'm bored. Call me back. Whatever.' He has no respect! You're not just some slut!"

I swallowed the lump in my throat and e-mailed Zack. "Like I told you, my parents are super strict, maybe don't call my house."

Zack took this to heart. The next time I saw him, it was a complete surprise. I had told him in passing about a play I was doing—a truly horrible "modern" "reinterpretation" of *Alice in Wonderland* where the White Rabbit was "DJ White Rabbit" and wore a clock around his neck like Flavor Flav—but I didn't expect him to show up.

"You did a great job," he said afterward, but he looked mournful. "Is your stepmother here? I want to apologize."

"Oh . . . I don't know, she's around here somewhere." I didn't want to subject him to her wrath. His sincerity caught me off guard. Did he really care that much?

He pressed something into my hand and said good-bye. It was a Pearl Jam mix CD. No one had made me a mix since I was four and my mother taped the New Kids on the Block songs I liked off the radio. Maybe I had the wrong impression of him. Zack played at being carefree and irreverent, but deep down he must have been what I had always wanted, a Sensitive Guy. There was nothing more attractive to me. He was deep and pained, I was newly fifteen and knew all about pain. We were perfect for each other. I had to give him another chance.

I saw him at a birthday party a few weeks later. While the other kids danced, he and I clustered in the corner with our friends Nicholas, Tim, and a girl named Sunny, a sweet model-actress-singer who was in a girl group called Knockout.

"You're like my sister, Sunny," Zack told her, and jokingly added, "My incestuous sister." She laughed and elbowed him. I was surprised I didn't feel jealous, but somehow I knew she wasn't a threat. He had a lot of beautiful girl friends, but rarely tried to date any of them. The last few girls he'd dated had been . . . well, girls like me. I was friends with most of them. And they all said he was an amazing kisser.

"Are you still auditioning, Mara?" Tim asked.

"Kind of," I said. "I was asked to audition for a pregnant

teenager for this show, but I'm going to be out of town when they're filming. It sucks. It could have been a really big thing for my career, you know?" By that point I was going to fewer and fewer auditions and wasn't even sure I had a career anymore, but I wanted to let him know I'd *almost* been cast as someone who'd had sex.

"Yeah, I have a big audition coming up," Zack said. "It's for the prequel to *Dumb and Dumber*, doesn't that sound awesome?"

"Yeah," I lied. If only I could talk to him alone. He was always joking, always so guarded, and he never made a move. I left the party disappointed.

But two weeks later it was Tim's birthday, and I knew Zack would be there. The party was at our other friend, Nicholas's, house out in the desert, which had a big backyard featuring those mainstays of teenage romance: a hot tub and a trampoline. I'd gotten there early, and when Zack walked into the yard, my stomach flipped. I had been sitting on the trampoline, telling everybody about "a weird kind of like psychic thing I can do: I can, like, read people's eyes." One day I had told my friend Arica she had the saddest eyes I had ever seen, and from then on I thought I had some sort of gift. My OCD had waned, and I no longer believed I could predict the future, but saying I had psychic powers seemed more funny and less self-aggrandizing than calling myself "observant."

Zack was wearing sunglasses. He had always reminded me of Brian from *The Breakfast Club* or Duckie from *Pretty in Pink*, but I was starting to think that if they ever made a remake of *Heathers*, he could make a great J.D.

"What about me, then?" Zack said, taking off his shades. I

looked him in the eyes and felt a jolt. They were so much more green than I remembered. He looked away.

"You're hiding something," I said.

He sat next to me, and didn't leave my side for the next four hours. We talked about his ex and my parents. We danced together, at least as well as two bad dancers could to Eminem's "Without Me." We went back out to the trampoline and told stories. He wanted to spend time with me, that was clear. But it was starting to seem like if I wanted him to make a move, I would have to do something drastic.

Zack was in the middle of a story about his improv group. "And I said yeah, 'cause, you know, I'm a man—"

"You're a man?" joked Tim.

"Well, I'm a half man," said Zack.

"Half man, half *animal*," said Nicholas, and once again I had an impulse.

"Animal, you say?" I pounced on Zack like a tiger. It was a stupid thing to say and probably even stupider to do, but suddenly he was in my arms and I was in his and he was not letting go. We lay next to each other, inching closer and closer together as the rest of the party left the trampoline, and a harvest moon rose up above us. As soon as we were left alone, I turned and threw my arms around him, holding him tight and feeling our hearts beat next to each other.

"I'm really . . . attracted to you," he said. I couldn't imagine anything more romantic.

"I'm attracted to you, too."

"GET A ROOM!" someone yelled, interrupting our reverie. Zack gave them the finger, but kept his other hand in mine, and kept it in mine for the rest of the night, while we went in the hot tub, while we ate cake, and while we watched a really terrible horror movie Nicholas had been in when he was two.

"This movie sucks," I announced, and everyone laughed. I was emboldened, drunk on infatuation. But was it going to move any further? Would my first kiss happen? (My first *real* kiss; I'd decided the whitewater rafting trip Spin the Bottle didn't count.) What if it wasn't good?

Suddenly it was bedtime and nothing had happened. The girls were sleeping in the spare bedroom, while the boys laid out sleeping bags in the TV room. The chaperones called for lights-out, and I sat in the dark, squeezed into a bed with Lauren and Maxine, until I couldn't take it anymore. I went back out into the family room.

"Zack?" I whispered.

"Yeah?" He stood up, a silhouette in the dark. I went to him, shaking with nerves and anticipation, and put my lips on his. It was a brief kiss, but one I felt through my whole body. The stories had been true: he knew how to kiss.

"Good night," I whispered, and ran off to the spare room again, where I wouldn't sleep for hours.

The parents who'd chaperoned the party knew about the trampoline and the hand holding and found the whole thing hilarious. I wouldn't know it until a few weeks later, but Tim's mom had called my parents the next morning, saying, "No need to come pick her up out here, we'll drive her back to the Valley, and you can pick her up at Zack's house." They knew Zack wanted to keep me around as long as he could.

That night my parents took me and my sister to Universal CityWalk, the outdoor mall at Universal Studios, and it was imbued with new beauty. The neon lights were as beautiful and pure as a sunrise. Buca di Beppo was the most romantic restaurant on Earth, making the Olive Garden look like . . . well, the Olive Garden. "I Think We're Alone Now" played on K-Earth Classics on the ride home, and it was about *us*. It was our song, though he would never know it.

Zack would have made fun of me if he knew. He would probably have rather had our song be "Black" by Pearl Jam. I knew we had some differences. He didn't like Weezer—he thought they were whiny and derivative—and I didn't like Pink Floyd—I found them pretentious and depressing. But we agreed on what was important, like racism being bad and Harry Potter being great.

"I think Zack likes you," my stepmother said a few days later, and I tried to look surprised. "At least he's leaving more polite messages on the machine now."

Later that week, Zack and I went out with a group of friends, but we stayed close the whole time, sneaking kisses when we could. When my parents came to pick me up, he asked my father if he could come out to dinner with us, and Dad said yes. Zack asked my father, the electronics engineer, about hard drives and defragmenting ("I Googled a lot of stuff the night before," Zack told me later), and they seemed impressed.

"You should come with us next week to Anna's dance recital," said my stepmother. "It's at the Pomona county fair!"

I wanted to yell "No!" but Zack said "Sure." He was willing to jump through my parents' hoops. The next week he sat in the back of the minivan, holding my hand. At one point, apropos of nothing, my sister turned around and said, "Mara's chest is really comfy, you should rest on it sometime."

"Anna, shut up!" I said, but Zack was amused.

"If she'll let me, sure." I was glad my stepmother didn't hear that.

Zack was a good sport, sitting through Anna's dance to No Doubt's "Hey Baby" and splitting Dippin' Dots with me. We kissed on a Ferris wheel and in the backseat on the way home when my parents weren't looking.

"So what *are* we?" I whispered. Entrapment.

"What do you mean?"

"Are we, you know . . ."

"I don't know," he said. My heart sank, but after a moment he said what I'd been hoping he would say: "Do you want to be my girlfriend?"

Yes, I did.

"This is just the beginning," my stepmother told me. "He's just the first one."

I didn't see why she had to say that. Yeah, maybe we wouldn't get married—maybe—but how would she know? She didn't get us.

"Something feels different with you," Zack told me, and I knew he meant it, because he also wrote it in his LiveJournal. "Different than it was with the others."

It didn't feel different to me, since I had no basis of comparison. It felt novel, a completely new kind of intimacy I had never even imagined. Zack understood me, and I thought I understood him, too. Both of us were sensitive and temperamental, so much so that sometimes we would put each other on "Moody Alert."

We talked a lot about our parents. I'd always thought his mother was cool, but when he told me she smoked pot, I started to think maybe she was *too* cool. Both of his parents were recovering addicts. A lot of child actors are children of addicts. Some of them are forced into acting: maybe the parents used to act themselves and feel like living vicariously through their kids is all they have left, or maybe they just need money. Other child actors, used to instability at home, and seeking the validation that comes with pleasing others, are drawn to it on their own. Sometimes an acting career becomes the most stable thing in their life, which is saying something.

Even if we never admitted it, we were both sick of acting. I wanted to be a writer, and what he really wanted to do was direct. Neither of us liked school, but for different reasons. The kids at my school were mean to me, and Zack just thought it was a waste of time. He had done what a lot of actors we knew did, and went to a special school where he could get his GED before he turned eighteen. He was now in college—L.A. Valley College, a community college, but still, I was impressed. Valley kids like me tended to be smothered by our parents, while L.A. kids ran free. He was part of that scene, playing at being a grown-up. Sometimes it could be a little intimidating.

"So I did something special for you," he told me on the phone one day.

"What did you do?"

"I deleted all my porn," he said, proudly.

"Oh," I said. I didn't watch porn, I found the idea of it unappealing and a little degrading, but I wouldn't have asked him to stop looking at it. Boys looking at porn was a fact of life. "So . . . you gave up porn for me?"

"No, I still watch it when I'm bored," he said. "I just don't have a bunch on my hard drive anymore."

"Oh," I said again. "Okay."

At some point, we were going to have to talk about sex. Before we had admitted our feelings for each other, I had once told Zack I was "celibate." ("Really? Me, too," he had said, "but not by choice.") The word "abstinent" didn't quite fit because it meant "waiting until marriage," and that seemed unrealistic—like waiting to eat dinner when you hadn't had breakfast or lunch, and you didn't even know dinner would definitely happen. I knew I wasn't going to have sex until I was ready, and I couldn't see being ready while still in high school. But I was starting to feel something new. I couldn't stop thinking about the day after the sleepover, before my parents had come to pick me up, watching Zack sitting on his bed playing his guitar, wearing a sexy pair of glasses I had never seen before. It was a tableau I would replay in my head later that week while taking an unusually long bath.

"I told this guy in my improv group about you, and he was so sketchy," Zack wrote to me. "I was asking him advice, and he was like, 'blah blah blah . . . then titty-fuck her.' I was like . . . a'ight."

"Yeah, maybe don't ask him for advice," I wrote.

"We can do or not do whatever you want," he wrote back. He knew I wasn't really "dirty." But I knew that on his first date with his first girlfriend, she had asked him, "So how far do you want to go?" and put her hand down his pants. He was used to dating girls who could do what they wanted, not someone who refused to let him touch her breasts, whose parents hovered over the two of them all the time. We could make out in my bedroom, but when we heard the thud of my father's steps on the staircase, Zack would leap off the bed and run to the other side of the room. By the time my father passed by the open door, Zack would be standing ten feet away from me.

I was not the easiest person to date. Even aside from my parents' many, many rules and my self-imposed chastity, relationships had rules I didn't understand yet. Being honest was important, I knew that, but maybe not my particular kind of careless, compulsive honesty. Once in a movie theater I asked Zack if he wanted a cinnamon Altoid. He said yes, I put it in my mouth, and passed it to him with a kiss.

"You want it back?" he asked a minute later, coyly.

"Hmm, no, that's okay," I said. He seemed a little hurt. What? I just wasn't really in the mood for an Altoid.

Later that night—in the food court—he had looked into my eyes, stroked my cheek, and whispered, "You're *so* beautiful...." And I had said, "No, I'm not."

He sighed, rolled his eyes, and in the same gentle whisper said, "You're *so* ugly."

We both had issues the other couldn't fix. I called him during a panic attack, and he didn't seem to know what to do. My depression had flared up at the start of the school year, and he was the only person I felt I could trust.

"You are the only good thing in my life," I told him.

"Oh, thanks," he said. "That's nice of you to say."

He didn't get what I was going through, or how to help me— not that many sixteen-year-old boys would have. But things weren't going well for him, either. He hadn't gotten the part in

Dumb and Dumberer. His mother had started smoking pot again, and he was moving out to live with his father.

"I thought you said you liked living with your mom more," I said.

"I do," he said, "but it's a really bad living situation right now."

I felt for him. I thought I understood him. So I didn't know what to do when, after he'd been away at a family reunion in Las Vegas, he instant-messaged me, saying, "Hey, can you call me? We need to have a talk."

That didn't sound good. "Is it bad?"

"No. Well . . . not *bad*, but not good."

When I called him, he told me he thought we should "take a break."

"What did I do?" I said.

"Nothing, I just don't have the time or money for a serious girlfriend right now," he said.

"I've never asked you to buy me anything," I said. He bought me a Weezer sticker at Hot Topic once, but that was on him.

"Yeah, but still," he said.

"So you're breaking up with me because of money?"

"I'm not breaking up with you," he said. "It's not the end. We'll kind of go back to the way things were before we had made it official, okay?"

"Okay . . ." I wanted to believe him.

"I feel so shitty now." He sighed, and I was suddenly angry.

"Yeah, well, that makes two of us," I said, and Zack began to sob. If it was just a break, if we were going to be the same as before, why was he crying?

"I'm . . . I'm sorry, Mara."

He hung up, and never called me again.

* * *

"So you guys broke up," said my stepmother.

"It's just a break," I said. "Not a break*up*."

"He doesn't call you anymore."

"We still talk online sometimes, and he picks up when I call him." I didn't mention that he never seemed to have time to talk—he always had somewhere to go or something to do.

"You were too alike," she said. Why did she have to use the past tense? "You're both moody, flighty people. Who's going to be the stable one?"

On this count, I knew she was right. Zack could get so angry and bitter over nothing. It was something I didn't like in myself, reflected back at me. He could just be rude, too. A friend sent me an e-mail chain survey, the kind you filled out with inside jokes and sent to friends. I sent it to most of my friends, and to Zack, too, even though we were "on a break." He filled it out and sent it back, which I wasn't expecting, but it was clear that he had only done it to make fun of me. Every other answer was "boobies" or "poon."

"Did one of your friends *really* ask what was better, sex or cupcakes?" he wrote. "Anyone asking that isn't getting laid."

Did that mean he *was*?

I turned to Zack's ex Maxine. She was fast becoming the Pamela Des Barres of teen actors: she had dumped Zack after she met Nicholas, and they had dated until she hooked up with another teen actor, one who had been a major character on a Nickelodeon show.

"I know he likes me," I said to her on AIM, "so why is he being so rude to me?"

"I don't think he *does* like you anymore," she wrote back.

My heart dropped. "What? Why?"

"He's dating someone else," she wrote, and I started sobbing. All I could do was ask who.

"I don't know," she wrote, "but all his friends say it doesn't look good."

I logged off and cried for a week. It hurt so badly, a completely new kind of pain I could never have imagined. I had been broken up with, and I hadn't even known it.

"It isn't good," confirmed Tim when I called him for more information. "She's *twenty-eight.*"

Twenty-eight? Zack was only sixteen—how could he even have met someone that age? His improv group was older, but it was all male. Maybe it was the woman he told me about whom he'd met in that support group for families of addicts. They passed notes to each other, and in one he had joked about oral sex being the solution to every problem. She had crossed out "oral" and written, "Why limit yourself?" Zack had laughed when he told me, but I didn't. I was uncomfortable. He'd shrugged and changed the subject.

"She's, like, kind of a hippie," said Tim. "She doesn't really believe in age." Or in California's penal code, apparently. But I didn't yet see it for what it was, an immature adult preying on a precocious teenager. I just saw him doing something drastic to get away from me, and being an evasive coward about it.

The closest thing to closure came a month later, once again through the Internet. Someone had decided e-mail surveys were passé, and now a Quiz Your Friends site was making the rounds, where people could build a little test based on their memories and inside jokes to judge their friendships. Right answers got a

"CORRECT!" and two points, and friends would be ranked at the end. Zack sent me his. I wasn't sure why he would do that—we hadn't talked in weeks—but I decided to take it. Most of the quizzes were full of minutiae like "What song did I get stuck in my head last week?" or "What color do I usually paint my toenails?" but there was a chance I'd actually get some insight into what he was doing and thinking.

The first few questions were innocuous, though I got fewer right than I had expected. But the final question threw me.

> 5. Who's my baby?
> A. Angelina Jolie
> B. Natalie Portman
> C. The girl from *Matilda*
> D. I can't tell you.

"The girl from *Matilda*?" I sat for a long time before choosing. It couldn't be me. With a sick feeling, I chose D.

"CORRECT!"

A wrong answer. That's all I was to him. And I didn't even merit a name.

"Fuck you, Zack," I said out loud. We were done. I was done. Tacky as it was, he had done me a favor: he had given me a reason to stop missing him.

In my late teens and college years, after I'd had my heart broken again and again, Zack became a kind of symbol. He represented all my relationship mistakes, all my misreadings and misconceptions. He played guitar, so he was an artist. He was an artist, so he was sensitive. He was sensitive, so he had to be *kind*. I think of it whenever I see a young woman fawning all over a nerdy guy, some comedian or actor, thinking he couldn't ever be cruel because he's funny and he wears glasses. He's not conventionally hot, so he's not full of himself, so he'll be a good boyfriend, right? I have Zack to thank for showing me that it often isn't the case. Guys like that always seem to think they're Duckie from *Pretty in Pink* when they're actually Steff.

national enchoirer

I NEVER HAD trouble making friends as a kid, but I did always have trouble keeping them. Every time I took time off from school to film a movie, I would come back to find my friends had grown and changed, moved on without me. I would eventually get back in sync, but it was hard. Half of childhood friendship is rehashing memories and inside jokes. "Remember when . . . ?" someone would ask, but I never did. I hadn't been there.

When I went back to middle school after filming *Thomas*, there was only one thing they'd all done that I hadn't: joined choir. It was all they ever talked about. But their passion went further than the Jordan Middle School choir room; it extended into a whole world I was about to discover.

"'Miss her, kiss her, love her . . .'" Alex sang one day as we worked on a science project. "'That girl is—'"

"'Poi-i-son!'" sang Sierra.

"I know that song," I said. "Who does it?"

"Well, Men at Work did it—"

"Oh, I know them," I said. "Aren't they Australian?"

They were incredulous. "No, it's one of the choirs at Burroughs. Didn't you go to Pop Show?"

And then it all came back to me. I had gone to Burroughs High School's Pop Show—a three-hour-long revue put on by the choir kids at their respective Burbank public high schools—back in 1997, when I was nine. I had been completely dazzled by the costumes, the music, and the synchronicity, and wanted desperately to be a part of it when I got old enough.

Show choir, as I understand it, started sometime after World War II in high schools in the Midwest. At that time, it meant girls with big hair and big smiles step-touching to Cole Porter songs while their male counterparts harmonized and pretended not to get the subtext. Show choir in Southern California at the dawn of the new millennium was something else entirely. The proximity to Los Angeles had changed it, as it changes everything.

L.A. isn't like Detroit or New Orleans; we don't raise famous musicians—aside from John Cage and Dr. Dre—but we do make them cool. We give them that Hollywood flair. And so it went with show choir: instead of show tunes and jazz standards, L.A.–area show choirs did pop, hip-hop, and R&B, all with their own brand of showmanship and fresh-faced teenage sex appeal (which was often as creepy as it sounds). In Burbank, Pop Show sold out every year, and would later air on the local public TV station whenever it wasn't showing city council meetings.

Suffice it to say that in my hometown, show choir was a pretty big deal.

So back to 1997. My friend's mother had an extra ticket for Pop Show, and I went along without knowing what it was. I had just wrapped *A Simple Wish*; film acting was starting to become routine, and I was feeling a bit disenchanted. The one idea that excited me, the thing I wanted to do more than anything else, was perform onstage. There weren't many opportunities to get involved with theater in Southern California, but here these kids were, performing live, wearing suits and sequins and giving their all—and I loved it. Not only were they singing some of my favorite show tunes, they were covering songs I'd heard on the radio! The girls who sang "Lovefool" and "Silent All These Years" sounded just as good as Nina Persson and Tori Amos. I gasped and clapped like I hadn't since I was four and my parents took me to *Disney on Ice*.

I was particularly taken with the Madrigals, Burroughs's all-women choir. Watching them in their red sequin dresses and twirly white skirts, bringing out the sweet in "You Don't Know Nothin'" and the sassy in "We Got the Beat," I knew I wanted to be one of them. This wasn't just a school club. This was a sisterhood, and if there was one thing I wanted more than to perform live, it was to feel free to be a girl. With my mother gone, my brothers and father ruled the house, and though they never directly made fun of me for being girly, I was always afraid they would. "Girl stuff" seemed both frivolous *and* complicated, and I didn't want to be seen as either. When I was a teenager, I promised myself, I would audition for choir, and I would get into Madrigals. It was my destiny. These were my people. This was performing. This was art.

That night I went to sleep in a haze and dreamed of sequins and spectacle. But when I went downstairs the next morning, Danny and his girlfriend Amy were on the couch, reading the Pop Show program and talking about how much they hated the choir kids.

My heart fell. I hadn't realized Pop Show was put on by the *choir kids*. I'd heard a lot about the choir kids from my brothers, and the stories were never good. They were the popular kids at Burroughs, but they were always getting into trouble. The homecoming queen was always in choir, but so was the girl who had to have her stomach pumped. They partied so hard it was scary. And they were also just cruel. All of my brothers had been ditched by friends when they joined choir, and so had Amy. Choir changed people.

I got the message: Choir kids were dangerous. I needed to stay away from them.

Three years later, I asked my friends if it was true.

"Do you think my sister Sophie is dangerous?" said Alex. "Or Dana? They're going to be in choir next year." Sophie and Dana were best friends. They got good grades and were nice. My brothers' theory was beginning to crumble.

"Dana got into Powerhouse!" said Sierra. "It's the best choir. No freshman girls *ever* get into it."

"Not even Sophie," said Alex. "She got into Mads."

"'Mads'? Is that Madrigals?" I said, and the yearning that had lain dormant in me for three years awoke. "They're good, too, right?"

"Yeah, they're the top *women's* choir, but it's not the same as getting into Powerhouse. There's also Sound Waves, which is mixed like Powerhouse, and Decibelles, which is all girls, but they're . . . you know. *Intermediate* choirs, not advanced."

They insisted on taking me to see Pop Show when it came

around again. By then we were in eighth grade, I was in choir with them—just regular choir; show choir wasn't offered till high school—and we actually knew most of the ninth graders performing. We couldn't get over how grown-up everyone looked. Sophie had a solo! Todd Ryder got *cute*! A fourteen-year-old girl belted out "making love was just for fun," and everyone was completely fine with it!

That sealed the deal: I *had* to be in choir at Burroughs. Performing with my elective improvisation and comedy class was one of the few things getting me through middle school, and soon I wouldn't have that anymore. Being onstage was the thrill I had been missing when I was acting in film. Besides, show choir was my destiny. My favorite movies were all musicals. My first favorite song as a child was Billy Joel's "The Longest Time," done a cappella. I harmonized along with the radio. The world needed more alto representation. The John Burroughs High School Vocal Music Association needed me.

*The Ethel Merman of
Burbank Temple Emanu El Preschool.*

Trying out for the VMA at the end of eighth grade was the most arduous audition process I have ever gone through, before or since. The choir director, Mrs. Ferro, was the Anna Wintour of the Southern California show choir circuit: an imposing figure who demanded excellence. The head choreographer, Renee, was equally terrifying. We had to fill out a form about our grades and character and sign another that said we were committed to the costs and rehearsals before we could audition. I fumbled through the dance portion, taking comfort that I would at least be able to match pitch on the "ear test," but I ended up fumbling through that, too. My "improvisation and stage presence" audition was inexplicably bad, especially considering my three years of improv classes. I didn't know why it was all going wrong.

Mrs. Ferro called it herself, after I finished my shaky sixteen bars of "Guys and Dolls."

"You're nervous," said a disembodied voice in the dark of the auditorium.

"Yes," I admitted.

"*You*, of all people, are nervous?"

I opened my mouth, but nothing came out. What I did on film, I wanted to say, I had the opportunity to do over and over again until I got it right. That wasn't possible onstage. Besides, the stakes were so much higher for this than for singing at the White House or performing the opening number of the Academy Awards. This was going to determine my social status for the next four years of my life.

The letter came on a May day, a month before middle school graduation. I opened it with shaking hands, holding the phone between my ear and shoulder as my friend Charlotte waited on the line. All I wanted was Madrigals. I knew I wasn't good enough for Powerhouse. And besides, I wanted that Pepto-Bismol pink sequined dress and that female camaraderie.

"I got into ... Decibelles."

The world seemed to get darker. Silly, stupid Decibelles. At the most recent Pop Show they sang a Britney Spears song. They weren't sophisticated women like Madrigals, they were *girls*. And they weren't very good: there were a few times at Pop Show when I couldn't even hear them singing. Maybe it was because I wasn't a good dancer, or because my voice was worse than I thought. Whatever it was, I felt like a failure. When I wasn't good enough for a part, I could avoid hearing about it, and I would never have to think about it again. This time, I would have to live with that knowledge for the next year.

Alex got into Powerhouse. Melissa was in Madrigals. It wouldn't be like middle school; we would never see one another in choir again. Our group of friends had been slowly disintegrating, especially after Melissa, Sierra, and I had all developed crushes on Alex, and now it was only going to get worse.

"Did you hear about Sierra?" Alex said on AIM the day after our final eighth grade spring concert. "Mrs. Ferro heard her 'Adelaide's Lament' last night and, like, *begged* her to join. She put her in Madrigals."

"What? Without auditioning?" My jaw was clenched so tight it hurt. That should have been *me*. That was supposed to be my spot. It was my destiny, and my best friend had taken it away from me. Sierra always got everything, and it wasn't fair. She was spoiled and always the center of attention. She was my best friend, and I hated her.

At the end of the summer we had a mandatory registration and workshop in the auditorium. I watched the returning Madrigals hug and air-kiss one another and wanted to crumple my choir dress measurement papers into dust. I was shaking. But I couldn't let my bitterness get the best of me. I knew I'd never make it through the next year if it did. If I couldn't make it into an advanced choir, I could at least be the best of the worst. Maybe make some new friends.

"What choir are you in?" I asked the sullen-looking ginger-haired boy beside me.

"Take a fucking guess," he said.

"Okay, Sound Waves," I said. He nodded, and I turned my attention to a cluster of Powerhouse guys standing a few feet away.

"Did you hear?" one of them said. "Matty got his first blow job this summer."

I shuddered. Alex's sister's friend Dana was in line nearby, about to fork over her parents' check for Powerhouse's standard three-hundred-dollar fee.

"Those guys," I said to her. "Are all choir guys like that?"

She laughed and rolled her eyes. Choir boys would be choir boys. "Wait till you have to change on the bus with them." I felt a rush of relief at having been placed with all girls.

"DECIBELLES OVER HERE!" yelled the head choreographer, Renee, and I followed a group of similarly young, dazed-looking girls into the auditorium's foyer.

"Okay," said our choir's president, a senior named Jackie. "We're going to go around the circle and say our names and why we joined choir."

"My name's Katrina," said a pretty blond girl. "I'm a freshman. And I joined choir because I want to be Britney Spears."

Everyone laughed, but I was horrified. I didn't want to be Britney Spears. I wanted to be Bernadette Peters or Idina Menzel, but I was starting to think no one here would even know who they were. No one here was even going to be impressed when I told them about the time Carol Lawrence, the original Maria in *West Side Story*, showed up at our house when my mother was sick and fed us home-cooked spaghetti and meatballs!

"I'm Olivia," said the next girl. "I'm a sophomore. And, well . . . I tried out for choir as a joke. I sang the Doublemint gum song. But I needed a fine art credit, so . . . here we go."

The rest of the girls murmured disapprovingly, but something stirred in my memory. Alex's sister Sophie had told me about a girl named Olivia. "She's the coolest. She's so funny, and she's such a good writer. She wrote this amazing Harry Potter fan fic you need to read."

"Well, I'm Beth," said the girl next to her. "I'm a sophomore, too. I was in Sound Waves last year, and I'm in Decibelles this year. I guess that's supposed to be an improvement." The girls murmured again. No one else had acknowledged that being in Decibelles wasn't good.

We were led outside to learn a dance, and in front of the auditorium was a banner I hadn't seen before:

JOHN BURROUGHS HIGH SCHOOL
HOME OF POWERHOUSE
2001 NATIONAL SHOW CHOIR GRAND CHAMPIONS

"We should rip it down," said Olivia.

"Yeah," said a sophomore named Karmeta. "Or deface it. Tag 'DECIBELLES' on it with purple spray paint."

They laughed, slightly bitterly, and so did I.

"Seriously, fuck Powerhouse," said Beth. Some of the freshman girls turned and looked at her sharply, as if she'd said something blasphemous, but I felt a warm feeling in my chest. I might have found my people.

I went home that night and looked up the fan fiction story, which it turned out Olivia and Beth had written together. It was the funniest thing I had ever read.

During the first few choir dance rehearsals, I stared at them from far away. Olivia had long, floaty hair, and lips permanently set between pursed and pouting. She looked like Patti LuPone in *Evita*. Beth was tall and bold, with a withering stare. I was both afraid and enraptured. Before I had dreamed about singing on Broadway, before I'd even dreamed of being an actress, I dreamed about being a writer. Olivia and Beth were living my dream.

We were supposed to be learning our choreography to the B-52s' "Roam"—how we ever got beyond licensing laws, I'll never know—but all I could think was how to get closer to them. If I could talk to them, I could be their friend, I knew it. The minute Renee's back was turned, I edged over. My heart was pounding. I felt like I was approaching celebrities.

"Hey, I read your story," I whispered to Olivia.

"Oh yeah? What'd you think?"

"I thought . . . I thought it was the funniest thing ever."

"Really?" She looked surprised, and for the first time, pleased.

"Back from 'Roam if she wants to'!" yelled Renee. She had

that condition unique to choreographers and directors, where they can listen to the same line or lyric thousands of times without ever getting it right. "Okay, so at 'around the world,' you're going to grab hands and get into a circle."

I wiped off my sweaty palms and took Olivia's hand. Maybe some of her coolness would rub off on me.

After rehearsal, I didn't think of going over my music or my dance. All I thought of was those two girls. Anything I could do to get in with them, I would do.

Even though Olivia and Beth were both sophomores, they were both altos, like me, and that created some camaraderie among us. Altos were just inherently cooler, not like those prissy, girly sopranos. Beth and I sat in the back because we were the loudest, and we would groan in unison when one of the other girls said something stupid. But it was weeks before I worked up the nerve to ask her where they were eating lunch.

"Out front, in front of the auditorium," she said. "Wanna come?"

I did. Karmeta sat with us, and so did two altos I didn't know very well, a loud girl named Alexandra and a quiet girl named Diana. As we settled in, Olivia pulled out a notebook.

"Okay, here it is," she said. "My list of Top Five Aging Hoochies."

"Aging?" I said.

"No—though I guess we're *all* aging," she said, looking briefly pensive, before returning to her smirk. "I said *Asian* hoochies."

"Oh, okay." My stepmother was Asian. I looked at Karmeta, who looked uncomfortable, but I didn't say anything. If it was a big deal, I told myself, Diana would have spoken up. She was Korean.

"And number one," said Olivia, "is Hillary Chu!"

"Ugh, she's *such* a hellhound," said Beth.

"She's a what?" I said.

"A hellhound," said Beth. "One of those assholes from Mads or Powerhouse who think they're better than everyone else, you know? Like Jessica Fenton or Stephanie Bauer—"

"Or that kid with the mullet," said Olivia, and Beth nodded.

"But why 'hellhounds'?" I said.

Olivia smirked. "Because if choir were Hell, and Ferro were Satan, and we were the suffering souls, *they* would be the hellhounds."

I immediately knew what she meant: They. Them. The other ones. The ones my brothers had warned me about, the sleazy boys and the stuck-up girls.

"You're right," I said.

I would never look at choir the same way again. I had found my people. We had seen the injustice inherent in the system, and what was there to do but start our own subculture? Yeah, we were in choir, but we were in it *ironically*. We would give it our all, put on our glitter and sequined dresses and sing "If You Could Read My Mind," but the minute we stepped off the stage we'd be rolling our eyes. We knew exactly how stupid it was. We were bringing choir down from the inside.

It felt good to make some new like-minded friends, especially since I was growing further apart from my old ones. Sierra and I had been fighting, and overhearing her say "Mr. Campbell is so-o-o obsessive-compulsive!" hadn't helped. She knew I had OCD, and I was shocked she'd be so insensitive. Alex and I didn't

SO CALIF PERF SHOW CHOIR INVT'L
April 26-27, 2002 • San Diego, CA
©Tri-Star

Anarchy in the VMA!
(Yes, that's me in the front.)

have any classes together, and he was already deeply entrenched in enemy territory as a member of Powerhouse. Melissa and I still saw each other in English class, but every time she talked about Madrigals I went white-hot with jealousy, especially after I found out they were doing the song "Bathwater."

"'Bathwater' by No Doubt?" I was furious. Of course *they* got to do a song by one of my favorite bands. Meanwhile, three of our five songs were just songs Madrigals and Powerhouse had done three to five years earlier. Long enough so that no under-classmen would recognize them, but not so long that hellhound seniors wouldn't complain that Decibelles "ruined" their songs.

"I forgot something in the choir room, and Jessica Fenton

and Karen Gruber were there eating lunch," I told my group at rehearsal. "They were playing their competition video from their freshman year in Mads and were all 'This is how "Dreamland" is *supposed* to be,' talking about how much better theirs was."

"What a bunch of bitches," said Beth. "We didn't *ask* to do their stupid fucking ballad."

At competitions, we joked and heckled all through other schools' sets, but we reserved our greatest contempt for our own choirs.

"Did you hear Powerhouse didn't even *place* at the Arcadia competition?" Beth laughed. "They suck this year! Even Burbank High beat them!"

"They're so totally bourgeois," said Olivia. I didn't know what it meant and I didn't think she did, either, but, then again, she had seen *Moulin Rouge* and I hadn't, so maybe she did.

"We don't hate *everyone* in Powerhouse and Mads, though, do we?" I said.

"Not *every*one," said Beth. There were ways to justify which people we hated. The cardinal sin was acting like they were better than everyone else, or even giving off the impression that they might *think* they were. Conceited people needed to be brought down. Like all teenage girls, we were part vigilante. Being annoying was also a sin, if a lesser one.

I started assembling a mental list of who I could like. "You know Becca from Powerhouse?" I would prompt, and wait for either "Ugh, she's the *worst*!" or "She's so annoying!" or "Oh, she's not a hellhound." Beth hated Stephanie, the dance captain, the most. ("She's so *fake*!") Olivia's nemesis was Brooke, a popular Powerhouse junior with a voice like a Disney princess.

"She's in my chemistry class and she always says the most conceited bullshit," she said.

"Brooke's always been really nice to me," Karmeta said.

"She's not nice deep down though," insisted Olivia. "I can just *tell*."

She was working on a story called "Escape from Choir Island," where a bunch of nonchoir kids washed up on the shores of an island ruled by the hellhounds. In it were inside jokes about Mrs. Ferro begging teachers to raise her star soloists' grades so they wouldn't be ineligible to perform, the music notes on the JBHS VMA logo being inspired by a riff from a porno, and the droll piano accompanist who was rumored to be having sex with the barely legal girls who had just graduated.

"It's going to be *fabulous*," she promised. Olivia was a satirist. It was her job to bring down the choir hegemony.

"What are you going to do when it's done?" I asked.

"Put it up on Choir Trash." Choir Trash was a notorious gossip forum where kids from Burroughs and all the schools we competed against posted about one another.

"It's not Choir Trash anymore, it's just ShowChoir.info." I knew it well: my name on there was "The Angsty One." "And they'll ban you if you flame anyone or make threats."

"I'll find a way around it," she said. She sent me a link the next day: she had registered under the name "National EnChoirer."

"Want to know the *real* truth about what goes on in choir? Specifically, Burroughs Powerhouse? Stay tuned...." Immediately below was a comment from a moderator reminding her that gossip and threats were grounds for banning.

As I saw it, Olivia was the ringleader. She cared the least while still performing the most. She could make relentless fun of our cheesy holiday concert adaptation of *The Nightmare Before Christmas* while still getting a speaking part.

"I can't *believe* you haven't seen the movie," she said.

"It came out when I was, like, five." I couldn't tell her I had been too scared to see it.

She had what I considered impeccable taste. Judging by her standards, I needed to stop watching *SpongeBob* and start watching *Invader Zim*. I needed to stop listening to the *Rent* cast album and start listening to *The Phantom of the Opera*. I needed to stop shopping at Claire's and start shopping at Hot Topic. She wore Converse with song lyrics written on them, and her AOL profile was a masterpiece, a mix of quotes from childhood movies like *The Goonies* and darker ones like "The masochist says 'Hurt me!' The sadist says 'No.'"

"Sophie quoted Brooke in her AOL profile," I told Olivia one day. Olivia and Sophie had been friends freshman year, so close they were, in Olivia's words, "like twins or something," but they didn't seem to spend much time together now that Sophie was in Powerhouse. "Isn't it weird that she did that?"

"Sophie's a double agent," she said. "She befriends the hellhounds so she can bring them down."

"Is that what we'll do if we ever get into Mads or Powerhouse?"

"Ugh, don't even talk about that," she said. I changed gears.

"You know Gabriel's screen name, right?" Gabriel was a Powerhouse tenor who performed his own soft rock songs at Pop Show, and insisted that people call him by his first and middle names instead of his surname. I thought he would be mildly cute if he deflated his ego and cut his mullet, but Olivia hated him. "What if we spammed him? Like signed him up for Viagra newsletters? Or foot fetish sites?"

"Oh my God, that would be *fabulous*," she said. Olivia had introduced me to sites like Rotten.com, Bash.org, and Something Awful, and she loved any kind of online prank. "We could call it Operation Mullet Mail."

We did that, and we did worse than that. I can't remember doing things like this with any of my other friends. I lived for the moments when she would stop and sigh and tell me a little about her crush on Neil, the Drama Club heartthrob, or the romantic life she wanted to live with him in Paris someday ("We'll have two kids, and one will always be playing the violin on our roof. . . ."). When she told me I was "a fabulous person," I felt warm in a way I hadn't with friends since middle school. What I had with Melissa, Sierra, and Alex must not have been real, or at least it wasn't anymore.

There was just one problem. Olivia already had a best friend: Alexandra, another antichoir alto. And I got the feeling Alexandra didn't like me. At lunch one day I asked her for her screen name.

"It's PopShowFan86," she said, rolling her eyes.

"What is it, really?" I said.

"I'm not telling you."

Before I could think, I said, "Why not?"

"Because I don't want you to talk to me."

"She says you *bother* her," Olivia told me when I asked her about it later.

"How?" I said. "What did I do wrong?"

"I dunno, she probably just thinks you're annoying." I felt like I'd been damned. Annoying was second only to conceited. Alexandra was trying to blackball me.

"Oh, don't take it personally," Olivia added. "It's not a big deal."

It was to me. The Fab Four, the Ace Gang, or whatever they were calling themselves that week, was only Olivia, Beth, Alexandra, and that girl named Diana. Karmeta and the other girls on the periphery of the group didn't seem to care, but I did.

Maybe Alexandra didn't like me because she thought I was moving in on her best friend—and in a way, I was. Olivia had told *me* about her crush on Neil before she told Alexandra, and I had gotten her to come to the Gay Straight Alliance meetings at lunch, and both her and Beth to audition for the Drama Club's spring play.

All three of us were cast and fit in immediately. It was so much more relaxed than choir and the people were more fun. "Why aren't we in *all* the drama shows?" said Beth.

"Why aren't we all in drama?" replied Olivia.

We shrugged, but we all knew the answer: Because drama wasn't *cool*. Because underneath, we did care about choir. Why else were Olivia, Beth, and I auditioning for the next year?

My parents didn't look happy when I told them I wanted to audition again. They didn't know what to make of show choir. They didn't like spending so much time and money, and they weren't sure about my new friends. Karmeta they had always liked, but they didn't seem to trust Olivia.

But they didn't tell me I couldn't audition, so I did, and this time, it went well. Mrs. Ferro said, "Very good, Mara, loved it!" after my audition, and she seemed to like me: I was a shoo-in for Madrigals.

We all figured Beth would make it, too, but Olivia didn't seem happy after auditions. She had sung "Because the Night" and Mrs. Ferro had stopped her and made her start again. Then she'd interrupted her and said it was "way out of tune."

"I'm so sick of her shit," Olivia said.

"Olivia is saying she might not do choir next year," I told Sophie over instant message. "She can't do that! What am I going to do without her?"

"What about what *she* wants, hmm?" Sophie replied. I didn't write back.

Alexandra hadn't auditioned at all, and though that wasn't as much of a loss, Karmeta hadn't, either. Her mother had forbidden her, saying choir was too expensive. The group was falling apart. I still screamed and jumped up and down when the letter came saying I got into Madrigals, but once I calmed down I immediately called Olivia.

"This doesn't make sense," she said. "Beth was put in Sound Waves, and I . . . I got into Madrigals."

"You did?"

"I did."

"So . . . are we going to do this?" I asked her. Were we going to stop worrying and love show choir? Run with the hellhounds?

"I guess I'll do it," she said, finally.

The next day in choir, Olivia looked conflicted and Beth looked morose. Mrs. Ferro addressed us at the end of class.

"Those of you talking about who should have gone where, I have one thing to say: you weren't in that room, and you didn't hear what I did."

"Ask her why you didn't move up," I said to Beth. She nodded and, as the room let out, walked up to Mrs. Ferro. The last thing I saw before I left was Beth saying, "I just want to know why . . ." and bursting into tears.

"It's not going to be the same next year," Olivia said, and I knew she was right.

Fall orientation was as exciting as auditions had been nerve-wracking. We were going to nationals in New York City! It was an open competition and we didn't have to pass through any prelimi-nary regionals or sectionals, but who cared? We had to be mea-sured for the legendary pink dresses—"salmon sperm," returning girls called them, after the unfortunate sequin swirl pattern—but also for the jeans and cowboy shirts we would rip off during our cover of "You Really Got Me." We got a costume change. This was the big leagues.

The upperclassmen girls were captivating. No one wore a training bra anymore, and some of them might not even have been virgins. In Decibelles, girls would say "I need a tampon" a little too loudly, giggling at their own bravado. Madrigals girls would ask a friend for a scented Super without any embarrass-ment. It was what I had suspected: Decibelles was for girls, Mad-rigals was for women.

It was what I had hoped choir would be, back when I was in middle school. It had to be too good to be true. And it was, though not in the way I was expecting.

Olivia had seemed a little distant since the summer. Where tenth-grade Olivia had been whimsical and charming, eleventh-grade Olivia was different, more dramatic. Bolder, but not always in a good way. The first time she came to my house that summer, she had told me, "Your house reminds me of a movie. I think it was *The Virgin Suicides*."

I could have shrugged it off if it hadn't gotten worse.

"I hope we do more four-part harmonies this year," I said to her.

"Why?" she said, smirking. "You want to feel *special*?"

"I . . ." Well, yeah, I did. I wanted some recognition for the Alto 2s. Of course I wanted to be special, it was why I was in choir. But now I felt ashamed of it.

Her look had changed, too: she had cut her long, floaty hair into a pageboy, and started wearing glasses instead of contacts. She even smelled different. We still sent e-mails back and forth and left notes in each other's music binder cubbies, but she started writing hers half in French, which she knew I didn't speak. The parts in English said things like "I wish I could stop manipulating people but it just feels so damn good."

I probably should have known to run at that point, but I thought I could get her back to how she had been, so I persisted.

I called her one Saturday in October, asking if she wanted to hang out.

"You want to meet up? Maybe go to the mall? Like in an hour, after my Alka-Seltzer kicks in," I said. "My stomach's a little jumpy, we went out for breakfast and there was ham in my omelet."

"Ugh, I don't understand why you still don't eat meat," she said. "I, like, *love* meat. More than anything else. There's got to be a word for what I am."

"Carnivore?"

"No, like, even beyond that."

"There *is* nothing beyond that," I said.

"Look, do you want to go to the mall or not?"

I played with the phone cord, finally asking, "Will it just be you and me?"

"If you want," she said, with a sigh.

My stomach tightened, and I heard myself asking, "Am I not your friend?"

"You are, but—"

"But I'm not in your clique," I said.

"Look, you kind of tagged along last year, and we liked you or whatever, but, you know, we were already, like, established."

My chest tightened up, too, and I tried to get the words out. "Well—I was . . . You know. I was fighting with my friends, and I didn't really have a group anymore. . . ."

"Well, that wasn't *our* problem."

I put my hand over the receiver and took a few ragged breaths, trying not to cry.

"You know, I don't really feel well," I said, finally. "I think maybe I shouldn't go out." I hung up, ran up to my room, and threw myself on my bed, crying. I had seen Olivia be mean to hellhounds, but I had never expected her to be mean to me.

Things didn't get better. We were going on one of the legendary choir retreats the next weekend. I had asked to share a cabin with Olivia, and now I was anxious about it. I knew for sure it had been a bad idea after she bumped me while I was brushing my teeth. When I complained about getting toothpaste on my shirt, she said, "Cry me a river, build a bridge, and get over it."

"Mara, you dropped your *granny panties* on Diana's bed," she called, loud enough for everyone in the cabin to hear. She watched me the whole time we played I Never, raising her eyebrows after I admitted I sometimes let my hands wander while lying in bed at night, and laughing a mocking laugh when I admitted that the first time I had made out with a guy, it had been in the back of my parents' minivan. When I couldn't take it anymore, and stepped outside to call home on a choir mom's cell phone, she called after me, "Oooh, calling your boyfriend?" Zack and I had just broken up.

The ride home was the worst part. Instead of being snide, she just ignored me. "Kayla, I love you," she said. "You too, Meg." She told everyone in Madrigals she loved them, except me.

It was my fault, I thought. It had to be. At some point I must have been annoying or conceited, and now I needed to apologize. Once I got home, I made her a homemade card, complete with pictures of meat I'd cut out from magazines, and slipped it into her music binder cubby. "Whatever it was I did," I had written, "I'm sorry."

She didn't say anything to me after class. I checked her cubby, but the note was gone. The next day I stood in front of her seat in the first row.

"Olivia?"

Her eyes met mine briefly, but she wasn't looking at me. She was looking through me.

"Sit down, Mara," I heard Mrs. Ferro say, and I trudged back to the top row, trying not to cry. Olivia believed she was not like "other girls." Other girls were to be treated with disdain at best and malice at worst. Somehow, I had become one of the other girls.

* * *

I never expected that being in a group with forty other girls could be so lonely.

I told myself it didn't matter. Who needed friends when I had show choir? I wasn't going to hide it anymore. I loved it. The smell of the hairspray, the roar of the backing band. The sequins and glitter and boys watching us change backstage. I mastered the box step and grapevine and the step in "You Really Got Me" our choreographer Angela called "the stripper move, but don't call it that because I don't want to get fired." Instead of criticizing them, I cheered on Powerhouse as they won first place over and over again at the competitions we went to. And when Mrs. Ferro told us she was starting an extracurricular a cappella group made of the best singers from Madrigals, I auditioned and made it in.

But no one liked me. Especially not Olivia, and especially not Sherry, a pretty soprano who bullied and mocked me relentlessly.

It wasn't that bad, I told myself. Sure, Sherry had told me she didn't like me to my face, but I had also heard her say, "I tried to be anorexic, but it's really hard!" She was just kind of dumb, the type of girl who wanted to be a hellhound but would never quite make it. She couldn't really hurt me. Nothing would hurt as much as losing Olivia.

After choir I went to geometry, where my slightly-too-cool teacher hadn't given us assigned seating. Someone had taken my usual spot near the front, so I moved back to the third row instead of the second.

"You can't sit there," said an eleventh grader named Mario.

"What do you mean?" I said.

"We don't like choir people here. Go sit somewhere else."

He and his friends laughed, and I picked up my stuff to move. Great. Now I was being bullied in choir and *because* of choir. I might have loved the singing and spectacle, but was it worth it?

Mrs. Ferro liked me, maybe she would put me in Powerhouse next year. But did I want to be in Powerhouse? I was never going to be one of the stars, getting the solos and dancing in the front row. Madrigals was already a time commitment—I was exhausted all the time—and Powerhouse would only be worse. Between the rehearsals and the travel, it was as if I were majoring in choir. But what was it preparing us for? I couldn't name one of the former choir kids who had gone on to be a pop star. Mostly they just came back to Burroughs and hung around the choir room. There are only so many roles in dinner theater choruses or in *Beach Blanket Babylon*.

"Why do I even bother?" said a girl named Aya, after the terrifyingly precise Bonita Vista High School Sound Unlimited beat us for the third time. She might have been speaking for me.

"Choir is such a cult." My stepmother sighed.

"It is not," I said, though I was starting to have my own doubts.

"Are you even sure you want to stay at Burroughs?" she asked. I never denied it, but I didn't want to go to Burbank High or Catholic school. There didn't seem to be any other options until I came downstairs one Sunday morning and found a brochure on the kitchen table for a place called Idyllwild Arts Academy.

"Dad, what's this?"

"Take a look at it," he said. I flipped through it quickly. It was a boarding school on a two-hundred-acre campus up in the mountains. Students could major in music, creative writing, and theater, while still taking academic classes. Its alums had been accepted to schools like the University of Michigan and New York University, places I had already been imagining myself going in two years.

"We've noticed something," he said, gently. "You're not happy at Burroughs. You only seem to be happy when you're performing."

Tears stung my eyes, but I didn't know why. I quickly decided I would audition.

Our trip to nationals in New York began the same week as the Iraq War. Sherry's parents were so afraid of terrorist attacks they wanted to keep her home, though, to my disappointment, they relented.

We had fun exploring the city, but ultimately it was not us but Middle America—in the form of a choir from Indiana—that won the day. Powerhouse came in third of six mixed choirs, Madrigals third of three all-women's. My parents picked me up from the airport, and once we were at the dinner table, I told them everything.

After ranting about how corrupt it was that the judges and winning choirs had all been from Indiana, I paused to catch my breath, and my stepmother handed me an envelope. There was a card inside, and written on the back in my father's handwriting,

I saw "... great opportunity for you." I put the card down and looked up at my smiling parents and sister.

"We got a letter from Idyllwild. You got in."

"I did?"

I let out the breath I felt like I had been holding for the past two years. Choir didn't seem important anymore. Even Olivia didn't.

After I left, I stayed in touch with some of the people I had known at Burroughs. Karmeta and I kept friends-only online journals, and I sometimes talked to a girl named Heather I had known in Decibelles. Late in my junior year, she instant-messaged me to say that she had traveled to nationals with the Madrigals, and that they had won first place. (Powerhouse had to be content with third.)

"Did they put up a banner in front of the school saying 'Home of National Champions, Madrigals'?"

"Well, no," Heather wrote. Women's choirs never seem to have the same clout as the mixed choirs.

No one at Idyllwild seemed to understand the appeal of show choir, and my friends at NYU just laughed when I brought out my old Pop Show DVD. But someone else was watching, and was impressed. It's now Burbank lore that Ryan Murphy found the John Burroughs High School VMA's videos on YouTube, and was inspired to start a show. *Glee* was an instant hit, and suddenly, everybody in the world knew about show choir. Powerhouse, now often called "the real-life *Glee*," was on *Oprah*, *The Voice*, and *America's Got Talent*. Jennifer Love Hewitt donated thousands of dollars to them. (Why she didn't give it to, say, a middle school in Detroit without a choir room, I'll never know.) I tried watching *Glee*, but it was too bittersweet. Darren Criss and Chris Colfer were adorable, but not enough to distract me from the painful memories.

"You got out when you should have," said Alex after we reconnected online in college. "Choir got crazy after sophomore year."

"Crazy how?"

"Like . . . drugs and orgies crazy."

He gave me all the details I wanted about what had happened and what everyone was up to now, and Facebook filled in the rest. Dana was an actress. Sophie was a musician and a comedian. Sherry had become, against all reason, a guidance counselor. Beth moved to Utah and got married, and Karmeta was a librarian. I stopped short of looking up what had happened to Olivia. I can only hope she's changed.

Mean girls come in all shapes and sizes. Some are blond cheerleaders, and some are Francophile brunettes who love Tim Burton and write song lyrics on their Converse. It was rarely the hellhounds who said anything mean to me; they expressed no real malice toward me other than the occasional eye roll. They were at the top and had nothing to gain by pushing me around. The ones who scared me, who still scare me, are the girls who see all other girls as competition, who see themselves as the persecuted ones, the ones whom the pretty and popular girls hate. When you believe you're persecuted, you will believe anything you do is justified.

My senior year at Idyllwild Arts Academy, I met a new girl

named Ashley. She was a thin, pretty blonde with big blue eyes. She sang a song from *Grease* for her audition, while the rest of us sang Sondheim. She talked about cheerleading the way I talked about show choir.

"Ugh, she's so annoying," said a freshman named Andi, who exclusively wore black T-shirts and flannel. "She was saying in Spanish how she always asks her parents *'Todos listos?'* before they go out. *'Todos listos?'*" she repeated in a high-pitched nasal voice. "She's just so dumb. Ugh."

"Huh," I said. Andi reminded me of myself, and not in a good way. I decided to be friendly to Ashley. She was never anything less than friendly back, but I started to worry as she drew further into herself.

"I talked with her the other day," said my friend Sarah. "She asked what was wrong with her, why no one here likes her, and I said, 'Honestly, honey? It's because you're too *normal*.'"

"That's never been a problem for me before," she had said, her eyes filling with tears. Ashley was sweet and kind to me until the day she had to leave the school because she had stopped eating.

A lot of men wonder what a woman wants. The answer is power. There are many ways to get it, but the easiest way is to tear other girls down. Any girl can play that game, but there's no way to win, except not to play at all.

As an adult, most of my friends are women, and most are performers. Most love to sing and dance and perform as much as I do, and many are comedians. I used to think I'd feel competitive when around other funny women, but that hasn't been my experience at all. Mostly it's been like finding out someone else speaks the language I made up as a child and thought no one would understand. They, too, have stories about falling under the sway of cool, older girls they idolized, and all the things the cool, older girls talked them into. And they, too, had that moment when they realized they were all the "other girls," and that every girl in the world is, too.

the matilda-whore complex

"I FEEL LIKE I've stagnated."

It was June 2010, and I was in my therapist's office. It had been a year since I had finished NYU, and all I wanted was to not repeat what happened the summer before.

My boyfriend Sam and I had broken up the previous January, and I had sunk into a deep depression. When I was busy with work or school I could stave it off, but after I graduated, I didn't have anything. Every day, I woke up with a feeling of dread, applied for jobs, remembered we were in a recession, curled up into a ball on my borrowed bed in my sublet room, cried, worried about what I was going to do with my life, and watched and rewatched a British teen drama called *Skins*. When I got sick of that I would play The Sims and make little people based on the *Skins* characters. There must have been days when I did more, but I have no memory of them. When I got fitted for contact lenses at the end of the summer, I quite openly asked my optometrist, "So what should I do when I cry?"

For nine months beginning that September I worked as an after-school teacher at an underfunded, overcrowded public school in the South Bronx, a place Jonathan Kozol had written about ten years earlier, where rats ran up the cafeteria walls and third graders pointed out the drug dealers on the roofs across the street. It was as disorganized as it was exhausting, and I couldn't face another year of it. I resigned at the end of May, and once again I was staring down a summer with no job, no creative projects, no boyfriend, nothing happening in my life besides a deep feeling of dread for the coming months.

"I wanted this year to be better," I told my therapist, "but I feel like I'm frustrated in every way. Financially, creatively . . ." I looked at the patterns in her rug before adding, ". . . sexually."

"Why not take care of both at once?" she said. "Channel your sexual frustration into something creative. Write something sexy."

"Uh, yeah, no," I said. "I don't think so. Not going to happen."

"Why not?"

"Because . . ." I struggled for the right words. "Because *someone* could *see* it."

My greatest fear was that *someone*, part of the amorphous public, people who'd never met me, would discover I had any kind of sexuality. I had been a part of many people's childhoods, and therefore felt I had to at least *pretend* to be a Good Girl for the rest of my life if I wanted to stay in their good graces. Even after I turned twenty-one, I ducked out of the way at a party if someone took a picture while I had a drink in my hand, and I had never kissed anyone without making them promise not to tell. It was paranoid, but not entirely unfounded. People on the Internet were despondent when they saw I had *breasts*. They did not want to hear me talk about sex. The Matilda-Whore Complex, I called it.

"You don't have to show it to anyone," said my therapist. "You can keep it to yourself, or just your writing group. You're still meeting, right?"

I nodded. My only solace in the months after graduation was a weekly meeting with my friends from Playwrights Horizons Theater School.

We had all been in the same advanced playwriting class, and

Acting in a play in college. I once sent this to a guy on OkCupid who'd asked for more photos of me. He never responded.

at the suggestion of our instructor, Jeni, had decided to keep meeting to write, read, and critique our plays. That summer we called the group Playwriting Summer Camp, and as we continued on into autumn I loftily started calling us the Playwrights of Playwrights. Aside from the name, I rarely had anything to contribute. When the meeting was over I'd retreat back to my room and back into myself. I tried to write, but it felt daunting. It took way too much effort to rise above the sinking feeling inside me at all times, let alone actually get something down on paper.

"I don't think so," I said again. "I wouldn't even know where to begin."

It had taken me years to finish my first play, *Sheeple*, and even showing it to my friendly, supportive group had been excruciating. I was not a real playwright. A real playwright *wrote*. Besides, what did I know about sex? Sam had been my first love, my first and only real sexual partner. Once my heart had healed a bit, I had tried to date, but never successfully. Before graduation I'd thrown myself at a funny, fresh-faced former evangelical Christian named Justin who had recently decided he didn't believe there was a God. I was hoping to get to him before he realized he was cute. Justin let me down gently, showing off his RA conflict resolution training, and I'd politely accepted it, then crawled into bed and had a panic attack.

After graduation I'd signed up for OkCupid and gone on dates with friendly, intelligent, nonthreatening men, and I managed to sabotage every one of them. Either I talked too much about my ex or said something even worse. When a date asked, "Do you want to stay over tonight?" I blurted out, "I hope my Nintendogs will be all right!"

Online dating was too risky, I decided. I wasn't so famous

that I'd immediately be recognized if I put up a photo, but I was known enough that it wouldn't have been impossible for *Gawker* or Perez Hilton to acquire a screenshot of my profile and write about it. "FORMER CHILD STAR CAN'T GET A DATE," I imagined it saying, with a bunch of "How sad!" and "Who cares?" comments under it.

Besides, I didn't *need* a boyfriend. There were people who lived their entire lives looking in vain for that other person, and I had promised myself I was not going to be one of them. I had read and reread *Fear of Flying* when I was seventeen, and what had stuck (besides the eventual horror at the casual racism of the 1970s, and my roommate Jill's annoyance that I had gotten her book moldy by reading it in the shower) was the phrase "People don't complete us. We complete ourselves." I shouldn't need someone else.

Needing and wanting were two different things, though, and a year and a half on, I was starting to want again. It wasn't anything I could talk myself out of. It wasn't logical, it was hormonal. I wrote down a description of every cute guy I saw on the subway. I lingered too long on friends' brothers' Facebook photos. I almost blurted out something embarrassing to my cute dentist— his last name being a euphemism didn't help.

"I guess I'll think about it," I told my therapist, and, like always, added, "Can I call you later if I need to?"

"You can," she said.

We ended our session and I walked downtown in the late spring rain. My friend Myko was in a play at Collaborative Arts Project 21, a workshop of a new musical. It was a retelling of "Little Red Riding Hood" where the Big Bad Wolves were online predators, but, Myko had promised, "It's better than it sounds." He was right. Some songs were good, some tropes were subverted, and I was impressed with the acting. Halfway through the first act, though, I got distracted. It was theater in the round in a black box, we were sitting on risers, and the cast had to move behind us. They were making way too much noise. Muffled thumps, whispering, moans and groans—what were they *doing* back there?

Immediately, my mind went to the worst possible scenario, and my imagination answered my own question. *Oh my God, what if they're . . .*

Living in a city means having heard lots of people have sex. The walls were thin in my college apartment, and my next-door neighbor, who did lounge covers of Lady Gaga songs, used to wake me up in the middle of the night with her operatic moaning. Every time they started up, I would turn my speakers next to the wall and blast Paul Simon's "Fakin' It" in the hope her paramour would get the hint. Some people wanted to be heard. Public sex was something else, though, something beyond my desires and comprehension, but while the risk of getting caught is not a risk I'd ever want to take, a lot of actors are thrill seekers and adrenaline junkies. It wasn't that preposterous, and it was funny. I could write this. I could even throw in a reference to what actors are supposed to say when told they have ten minutes before they need to go on, and call it *Thank You Ten*.

The next morning, I sat down on my futon couch with my terrible old PC, and started writing a play where two people had sex backstage during the performance of a play. I knew right away it had to be set during *A Midsummer Night's Dream*. I'd been in it twice, first as a fifteen-year-old, playing a gender-swapped Egeus in an eighties power suit, then getting lucky and playing Puck when I was seventeen. It was familiar to me and to the rest of the world, something even people who didn't spend their free time discussing their love/hate relationships with Jason Robert Brown and David Mamet could appreciate.

It was also partly inspired by real life, though real life was much tamer. When I was eighteen, I couldn't imagine anything more romantic than two lovers reciting Shakespeare to each other. I broke away from making out with Sam one day to say, shyly, "Do you think you could recite Shakespeare to me?"

He laughed, but being a guy who had taken his AOL Instant Messenger screen name from one of Hamlet's soliloquies, he had no reason to say no. Sam dutifully began to recite his lines from *Much Ado About Nothing* between sloppy, frantic kisses. He had not been Benedick or Claudio or one of the sexier characters; he had been Dogberry.

"'Dost thou not suspect my place? Does thou not suspect my years? O that he were here to write me down an ass!'"

The backstage setup for my play was simple: he's waiting for his part offstage, she enters and, not knowing he's there, accidentally starts changing in front of him. He's more embarrassed than she is. It would be funny, I told myself, even though it was starting to sound less like a play and more like a story found in particular forums, the kind starting with "I never thought this would happen to me. . . ."

The characters came to me too easily. She was playing a fairy and he a mechanical, and they were both disappointed with their parts. She doesn't believe she's pretty or talented enough, he's nervous and overthinks everything. The two constant voices in my head, on paper. Anyone who doesn't think fiction is as revealing as nonfiction is wrong: it's *more* revealing, because the revelation is done unintentionally. Vince and Dulce—"victorious" and "sweet," respectively, because nothing is sexier than etymology—were getting more naked, and so was I.

I couldn't write this. This was supposed to be a backstage screwball sex comedy, not a therapy session. And not a letter to *Penthouse*.

It was ninety-three degrees and humid outside, but I needed a cup of tea. Tea calms me down in all weather. Too jittery to sit back down and try again just yet, I took a breath and put in my earbuds. A familiar bass line thumped through: "REACH OUT AND TOUCH FAITH!" For days, I had been listening to nothing but eighties New Wave. It made me feel better than my previous choice (the new Broadway cast of *Company*), and on some level I believed cheesy music wasn't cheesy as long as it was British. It was the same reason I could excuse binge-watching *Skins* while looking down on my friends who loved *The O.C.* and *Gossip Girl*. This belief in the inherent sophistication of all things British was connected to another common American misconception, the one I and every other girl who had a poster of Legolas on her bedroom wall when she was sixteen had committed: mistaking a British accent for a personality.

An hour later, I hadn't made much headway with the play. I was still typing with a hand over my eyes, too embarrassed to see what I was writing. Tea wasn't helping. Music wasn't helping. Nothing was helping. What I needed was not my own personal Jesus but my own personal muse.

Just then, my phone buzzed. It was Luke from my writing group.

I didn't know Luke very well, but I liked him. He had the same kind of intensity I did, the same neurotic sense of humor, and he wore glasses like Rivers Cuomo or Elvis Costello. The first time

I saw him, it was at a college festival of ten-minute solo pieces. His required him to dance around like an idiot to both Prince and Queen. Immediately there was a flutter in my chest, but I had a boyfriend, and feelings like that were dangerous. When it was time to give feedback, I'd been overly critical, trying to quiet any stirrings in myself. Luke had done the thing I found most attractive in a man: been willing to embarrass himself. This, I've learned, is a problem, as never actually feeling embarrassed is also a symptom of psychopathy.

But Luke was not a psychopath. He was nice, and smart, and he was also one of Max's Roommates. My friend Max had lived with seven different guys since we first met, and I'd had crushes on at least five of them. They were all so easy to project my dreams onto. After a while, the crush would fade, usually due to a Tragic Flaw I'd identified in him, some reason it would never work. He was too much like me, he was not enough like me, he was too religious, he was an actor, he was a musician, he called Williamsburg "Billyburg." Still, the allure held, my own hot-hand fallacy, as if Max—a former brief crush himself—was a catalyst for some kind of attractiveness. Being a straight single woman with a lot of straight single male friends became a probability word problem. *Which of these could make a pair?*

I picked up the phone. "Hey, Luke!" I said, a little too eagerly.

"Hey, Mara, are you free tonight?"

"I'm always free," I said, and cringed, though it was usually true.

"You want to go see Shakespeare in the park with me?"

"Whoa, you got tickets to Shakespeare in the Park?" I said, impressed. People waited hours in line for that. And he was asking me?

"Well, no, it's not Shakespeare in the Park, it's *a* Shakespeare in the park," he said. "It's a group my friend is in. They're doing *Richard III* on the Upper West Side part of Central Park."

"Oh," I said, mildly disappointed but still interested. "Sure, I love *Richard III*." Despite my squeamishness in all other aspects of life, I love violent Shakespeare. It is to me what steak is to some people: the bloodier the better.

"Great," he said. "I love it, too. One of my favorite Shake-speares."

And suddenly I was thinking how good Luke would be in the part of Vince.

"I'll meet you at the Ninety-sixth Street and Central Park West entrance at four, then?"

"Yeah, sure," I said.

Only after hanging up did I remember I *wasn't* free that night. Allison, my roommate and best friend from Idyllwild, was coming to New York, and I was supposed to see her. Allison was one of my favorite people in the world. She was open-minded, endlessly kind, a true and loyal friend. She was also a badass: she had scaled mountains in Nepal and led kayak tours in Glacier Bay. Despite her doing all kinds of things I would probably kill myself trying, New York could be a little overwhelming for her. She wanted me to show her around, and I wanted to see her.

It would end early, I told myself. I would still see Allison. It wasn't like I was going on a date.

The hour-long train trip from the East Village to the Upper West Side gave me ample time to worry. Being on my own with one other person has always made me nervous. It's not like being in a group, where I can just be funny and charming and put on a show. When I'm alone with someone, I have to be myself. It's too much pressure. No wonder I was bad at dating. My hands were shaking all the way from Astor Place to Ninety-sixth Street. It would be okay, I told myself. It wasn't a date.

Luke was waiting for me, wearing a backpack and a Duff Beer T-shirt. He looked good, and he looked happy to see me. I gave him an awkward hug and he led me to a grassy patch where a group of people was split evenly between sweaty actors in Elizabethan costume and sweaty onlookers in shorts.

"So how did you hear about this?" I said.

"I know the fight choreographer."

"Oh yeah?"

"Yeah, I've been thinking about asking him for help with a day job. He's a personal trainer, and they make good money."

"Oh, cool." His shirt suddenly seemed too small. I looked away, and tried not to think back to the show we had both worked on that January. It was a very loose adaptation of the myth of Orpheus, so loose that we had a Russian ballerina, multiple men in drag, and a band of shirtless guys playing glam-rock-inspired songs about designer drugs. Luke was in the band. I was the dramaturge, the person who did research and editing, which meant I had done most of my work before the show went up. All I needed to do on show nights was drink wine in the back of the theater, take sporadic notes, and try not to ogle the band. Six years of art school had made me immune to the seductive charms of a guy with a guitar, but Luke with his shirt off was a sight. Muscles were never what did it for me: most of the guys I had dated had been about six inches taller than me and about two pounds heavier. Still, looking at Luke, who had muscles I hadn't known existed, elicited a kind of unconscious lizard brain response, a reminder that my libido was just dormant and not dead. *Right, I'm a straight human woman. I like this.*

"So . . ." My chest tightened and my tongue seemed to seize up. If I didn't think of something to say, quickly, we would either be doomed to silence, or I would end up blurting out something way too stupid or way too personal. Small talk was hell.

He rescued me. "So you're showing stuff at our next meeting, right?"

"Uh, I don't know," I said. "Maybe."

"Oh. I thought you'd said you were going to."

"I said I'd do that?" Probably one of the sentences I had said most in my life. "I mean, I am working on a play right now, but . . . but I'm pretty sure it sucks."

Luke laughed. "You say that about everything you write."

"That's true," I admitted. "I think people think I'm a lot more insecure than I actually am."

"You do wear it on your sleeve," said Luke, but he was smiling.

"Yeah, I'm starting to think I shouldn't," I said. "I don't think it's as endearing as I once thought."

We settled down into the grass, and the actors took their places in front of us. My eyes passed over the rest of the crowd, and I felt myself tense up. I looked at Luke, then back at everyone else. We were the only two people there alone who were not holding hands.

Oh, shit. Was this a date?

"'Now is the winter of our discontent / Made glorious summer by this son of York . . .'"

I wasn't watching the play. I was watching Luke's knee. If he moved it closer to mine, did that mean something? Did I *want* it to mean something?

"'Was ever woman in this humor wooed? / Was ever woman in this humor won?'"

He wouldn't have invited me just as a friend. Or maybe he would have. I would have asked a guy just as a friend, but then, I would never be so confident as to ask one out on a date at all. My overture to Justin had been a colossal failure, and I generally assumed a guy was gay until proven straight, taken until proven single, and not interested until he'd put his tongue in my mouth.

Would we even make a good couple? Luke and I were a lot alike, but that might not be a good thing. I wrapped my arms around myself, wiping my sweaty palms on my sweaty tank top. I had been holding my breath since Richard's opening monologue.

"'Alas, why would you heap this care on me?'"

I looked to Luke. His eyes were on the actors. He was not moving closer.

It wasn't a date.

My relief was quickly replaced with disappointment. Of course he didn't want to date me. I was too nervous and not pretty, talented, or cool enough for him to be interested in. Or worse, this was supposed to be a date, but I had ruined it. He had noticed how uncomfortable I was and taken that as lack of interest. He didn't understand what I felt about him, but I couldn't blame him. Neither did I.

He would join the ranks of my platonic male friends, the ones with whom I could hypothetically share a small bed and do nothing but sleep. Many ex-crushes had become those. Max had been one. Myko had been one. We could be honest and intimate in a nonromantic way. Those friends were important to me, sometimes even closer to me than Sam had been.

Why, then, did I feel so bitter? Partly because bitter was my default state of being, but also because I *liked* having a crush.

211

Crushes were placeholders. They gave me hope. It wasn't fair to the person I had one on to place those expectations on him, but it was the way my mind worked. I couldn't help but make up stories to make myself feel better.

In books and movies there's always someone moaning, "I'm in love with him, but he doesn't even know I exist!" They've got it all wrong, though: it's not that the object of affection doesn't *know* you exist, it's that they don't *care*, which is much worse.

"'I shall despair. There is no creature loves me . . .'"

The play ended as the sun set. We sat in silence for a moment.

"Well, thanks for joining me," said Luke, finally.

"You're welcome," I said, unfolding my arms, standing up, and then folding them again. "Where are you headed now? I have to meet up with my friend Allison in a bit."

"Do you have time to eat first? My friend Mike wants to go to an Indian place, you know, like one of the ones on First Avenue. His roommate Michaela is coming, too."

Two other people, a friend thing. Safe.

"Sure," I said. "I'll tell her to meet me there."

We walked to the station and got on the train. I still couldn't look him in the eye.

"So what's the play you're writing?" he asked.

"Oh, it's really dumb. It's . . . a backstage comedy, I guess. Are you working on anything?"

"Yeah," he said. "My play's about a cannibal."

". . . Okay." I shouldn't have been surprised. Our writing group had already tackled abortion, euthanasia, conspiracies, statutory rape, incest, suicide, fratricide, patricide, and mass murder. There isn't a controversial issue or major human taboo that hasn't been tackled by a college-age writing group.

At dinner, his two friends sat across the table from us, and from the moment we ordered, they immediately started making out.

"Did you know they were dating?" I whispered to Luke.

He shook his head. "Nope."

My tolerance for public displays of affection is inversely proportional to the time it's been since I engaged in one. Luke and I made polite, uncomfortable discussion over our respective chicken tikka masalas until my phone buzzed. Allison. "I have to go," I said.

"We'll go, too."

When we got outside, Allison was standing there, and with her were three guys I had never seen before. I hadn't been expecting her to bring anyone else, and at first I was a little disappointed. If there was one person in the world I felt comfortable being alone with, it was her, and I valued that time. But my disappointment faded as I got closer and noticed all three of them were extremely cute.

She hugged me, then introduced me to Jesse and Oran, who were warm and friendly and, I assumed, both gay. "And this," she said, nudging a tall, tan, totally adorable, smiling guy, "is Gavin."

"Hey, how are ya," he said in an accent I couldn't place, and there went that flutter in my chest.

"Um, I'm fine," I said.

"We're gonna go, Mara," I heard Luke say.

"Okay, great," I said, and felt a guilty rush of relief.

We turned to walk the other way, Jesse and Oran walking ahead, Allison and Gavin on either side of me. His was a more obscure British accent, or maybe Australian. *No, no, no, don't do that. Don't fetishize him.* It was too late. He spoke and I was sixteen again.

"So . . . where are you from?" I said, trying not to sound shy.

213

"S'theffrikeh."

"Sorry, where?"

"S'the*ff*rikeh."

I must have looked bewildered, because Allison said, "He's from South Africa."

"Oh," I said. "So that's South African for 'South Africa.'"

Gavin took a few steps ahead, and I tried not to watch him go.

"How do you know these guys?" I asked Allison.

"Oran I've known forever, and I know Jesse through Oran. Gavin's been working with me at that camp upstate."

"Are the two of you . . ." I started to say, but she went on.

"He's become like my little brother the past few months," she said. "I love him even when he's a pain in my ass."

"What did you say about me?" Gavin said, turning around.

"I said you're a pain in my ass," Allison said, smiling at him. "But I love you anyway."

Allison wanted to see a jazz group perform on the Lower East Side, and I led the way. Jazz concerts reminded us both of Idyllwild, where the music majors who hadn't devoted themselves fully to orchestra would hold concerts and coffeehouses. Before Idyllwild I hadn't thought I liked jazz, but seeing it live as a hormonal sixteen-year-old had made me realize how sexually charged it was, and given me a new appreciation. With Allison, listening to jazz, and sexually frustrated. Not much had changed, I thought, staring at Gavin.

He was cute. Maybe not a hunk, but definitely too cute for me. When a guy was cute, I immediately assumed there was no way he could be interested in me. "Looks are the last thing I look for," I'd tell my friends. "I'm not really into conventionally hot guys." It was partly true, but more the case that they weren't into *me*. Or at least that's what I believed. In my mind, I was still the awkward twelve-year-old no one would ever admit to having a crush on. The lost token female geek from *Freaks and Geeks*, or a less endearing, less empowered Tina Belcher.

"We have to get back," Oran said to Allison as the concert ended. They were staying with friends in Jersey and it was getting late. Late for visitors, anyway. It was a little after midnight, only about nine o'clock New York time.

"Are you all going to go?" I said, looking them over and lingering a little too long on Gavin. "I have a futon, if you need one."

"Can I stay with you?" said Allison.

"Of course," I said.

Allison and I walked home together, planning our girls' night as we went. We'd eat cookie dough and play backgammon, like we did when we were roommates. Instead, when we got back to my apartment on St. Marks Place, Allison ended up listening to me rant about the state of the theatrical arts, just like she did when we were roommates.

We talked about the people she had been seeing. There didn't seem to be anyone serious in her life, but she was happy with that. Happy with herself, and happy with having options.

"I don't think I could do that," I said. "I need to know where things stand." Lots of my friends dated around or had open relationships, but I remained stubbornly and singly devoted to monogamy. Being with just one person didn't seem dull to me, but then, I had been the kind of kid who was excited to open the lunch she'd packed herself.

We decided we'd meet up with the guys again the next day and said good night. Every other night I would lie in bed thinking of what I'd done wrong that day, all the ways I'd mortified or disappointed myself. But that night, there were too many other things to think about: the play, Luke, and what might happen tomorrow with Gavin. I fell asleep somewhere been humiliation and hope.

The next day, we met up with Oran, Jesse, and Gavin in Chinatown at noon, and walked through Little Italy eating gelato. We went to the Evolution store and dared one another to eat cheese-flavored dried maggots. We went to Babeland and dared one another to buy vibrators. It was a movie montage of a day.

"What do you guys want to do tonight?" I asked over dinner. "Do you know any good bars or clubs?"

"Um, there's the one Irish pub I go to a lot. . . . Actually, I don't really know many."

"Jesse knows somewhere we can dance," said Oran.

"Yeh, let's go there!" Gavin said.

"He's so cute," Jesse whispered to me when Gavin's back was turned.

"He is," I agreed.

"Shame he's straight," he sighed, wistfully.

"So he's definitely straight?" I said, and Jesse laughed.

The place was on Fourteenth Street, half hole-in-the-wall, half hipster enclave. Someplace I should have known from my years at NYU, but hadn't. College is wasted on the cautious.

New Order's "Temptation" was playing. As soon as we pushed through the crowd, Gavin leaped onto the dance floor, a kid cannonballing into a pool. I hung back, in awe. The flutter in my chest was back, and it was not leaving. He didn't care if he was embarrassing himself. He might not have been the best dancer there, but he didn't care. He was having fun. He was fearless.

"Look at him." I sighed to Allison. "I couldn't do that."

"Sure you can," she said as Oran and Jesse joined Gavin. "Go. Go dance."

I wavered a little. "He's not a psychopath, is he?"

Allison did what she always did, what I loved her for, and took me seriously. "No," she said, gently, "he's not. Now go!"

I stepped onto the edge of the dance floor, a kid dipping her toe into the shallow end. "Temptation" faded, and on came a familiar baritone.

"REACH OUT AND TOUCH FAITH!"

Gavin whirled around, smiling at me. "Come on!" he said, and when I didn't move, he took me by the hand and pulled me, farther onto the dance floor, and closer to him. My hands were sweaty and shaking, I knew, but he didn't seem to care. After a moment, neither did I.

Depeche Mode turned into Tears for Fears which turned into Dexys Midnight Runners which turned into Elvis Costello. Eleven o'clock turned into two in the morning. Allison went to move the car, and everyone else went with her to smoke. I ordered a beer and sat on a couch near the door. Gavin joined me.

"You don't smoke pot, either?"

"No, I don't," I said. "I'm high-strung enough as it is, so I just know it'd make me paranoid."

"Yeh, I got really paranoid off it once a few years ago," he said. "I ended up in my mum's room at one a.m., like, 'Mum, I'm tripping balls!'"

We laughed and joked, and to my surprise, I was feeling comfortable.

But then a hot young hipster couple squeezed by us, and I was suddenly very conscious of my Old Navy tank top and jeans.

"I wish I'd known we were coming here," I said. "Then I would have dressed up."

"No, you look good," Gavin said, a slight smile at the corners of his mouth. He leaned back, and took another look at me in a way that made me shiver. "You look good."

Our knees were almost touching. Once again, I thought about moving mine closer. It wasn't like this guy would be my boyfriend. Even if he didn't live two hemispheres away, he had Tragic Flaws, too: he was younger than I was, he thought *300* was a good movie. But he was cute and nice and funny and fearless, and I kind of wanted his mouth on mine.

Allison came back. She smiled at me and Gavin, then said to him, "It's later than I thought. We have to get going."

"Oh," I said. "Yeah." Gavin and I looked at each other for a moment. I waited until he got up, then followed. We left the bar, and I went around the circle, telling Allison I loved her and hugging Jesse and Oran good-bye, but stopping when I got to Gavin.

"It was really nice to meet you," I said, looking up as he smiled down at me. I was up on my toes, reaching out. . . . Then I moved my arms down to give him a hug.

I walked back down Third Avenue by myself, alone except for everyone else in the city.

"Do you have a cigarette?" asked a passerby.

"No," I said. "But I have three different kinds of asthma medication."

It had been a good day, but something felt lost, unfinished. *Whatever*, I thought. Tomorrow was another day. Tomorrow I'd wake up, try to write my play, send some résumés out, and inevitably end up listening to Depeche Mode and reading the TV Tropes page on *Skins* again. Maybe something interesting would happen. Probably not, but I would live.

Back on St. Marks Place, I went upstairs, changed into pajama pants and a camisole, and put my hair up in a ponytail to keep it out of the way as I washed my face. I caught my reflection in the mirror.

"You look good."

If only he could see me now.

While I was taking out my contacts, my phone buzzed. A text from Allison.

"What's your address?"

Huh. I typed it in, adding, "Why?"

"Gavin forgot something."

Forgot? He hadn't even been to my apartment. Before I could think, the downstairs buzzer went off, and I clambered downstairs, barefoot and nearsighted, my heart starting to pound as I entered the foyer. He was there, in between the two sets of glass doors that led to the street.

"So . . . Allison says you forgot something?"

"To do this," he said, and kissed me.

I thought my legs would give out. He had me up against the cold tile wall, his hand on my shoulder, then my waist, then my thigh, and I could hear passersby on the street saying, "Oh my *God*, don't you hate it when people make out in public like that?" And I wanted to turn to them and yell, "SHUT UP! SHUT UP! YOU DON'T UNDERSTAND, THIS *NEVER* HAPPENS TO ME! NEVER!" and that even if it did it wasn't any of their business, but I didn't really want to because that would mean breaking away from kissing him and I didn't want it to end. But finally it was all too much and I opened my eyes and broke away and said, "Wait, what's going on?"

He looked confused. "I . . . I thought you were giving me signals at the bar."

"Oh, I *was*," I said. "But I didn't expect you to *do* anything about it."

He laughed, looked me straight in the eye, and said, "You are the coolest girl I've met in America."

I took a deep breath and said, "Do you want to come upstairs?" And he did.

"As soon as we got in the car," said Gavin forty minutes later, as we lay entwined, "I said, 'I should have kissed her!' I kept saying it, and finally Allison said, 'Well, go back, then! Tell her you forgot something, then when she asks what, kiss her.'"

"'And we'll drive off if it looks like it's going well'?" I said. He nodded and laughed, and I laughed, too. In the preceding thirty-six hours, I realized, I had laughed more than I had in the past year.

"I have to go," he said. He sighed, looked me in the eye, and said, "You are the coolest person."

"Thank you," I said. Any other time I might have qualified it or denied it, but instead, I just accepted it. Gavin leaned forward to kiss me again, squeezed my hand, and got up off the bed. I watched as he put on his shorts, and I knew I would probably never see him again.

"Hold on," I said. "Before you go, I have to ask you something."

"All right," he said, pulling his shirt on over his head.

"Did you ever see the movie *Matilda*?"

* * *

It was noon when I woke up. There was a Durex wrapper on the nightstand and a hickey on my neck.

"Oh my God," I said out loud.

Pulling on my robe, I went to the living room. The apartment was empty.

"Oh my God," I said again, to myself, and to no one. I needed a cup of tea.

For an hour I sat on the couch, curled up into a ball, sipping my tea. *What the hell have I done?* Something I never thought I could. Something someone pretending to be a Good Girl would never do.

I looked out the window. At some point, I was going to have to face the truth about how I was feeling. The truth was . . . I felt great. Alive. Desired. Confident. The wave of shock had washed over me. Someone cute and fun and fearless had thought I was cool. He thought I was sexy.

Maybe I could be. Maybe I was.

Smiling to myself, I reached for my computer.

"Okay," I said to the Playwrights of Playwrights a week later, "so this is a ten-minute play I wrote a few days ago. It's kind of ridiculous, but . . . you know what, I'm not going to apologize for this. Could Chris read stage directions, Annie read Dulce, and, um, Luke read Vince?"

They did. Annie and Luke tried to keep straight faces, while everyone else laughed and applauded, especially at my favorite stage direction: "Dulce reaches under her skirt and does something that makes him stop talking."

"'Bring him away. Oh that I had been writ down an ass!'"

At the end, when Dulce goes onstage as the audience cheers, my own audience clapped and cheered, too. I had never seen any of them react like that to anything I had written.

"I just realized something," Myko said to me. "You *really* like sex!"

I smiled and shrugged. "Most people do."

"I only have one note for you," said Chris. "You need to do a quick rewrite and fix anything you're going to fix as soon as possible, because you need to send this out."

"You think so?" I said. *But what if someone sees it? And knows that the girl from* Matilda *wrote this?* To my own surprise, I realized I didn't care. If anything, I wanted them to see it.

"Yes," said Annie. "Send it out." Danny, Max, and James all nodded their heads in unison.

"Great casting, by the way," said Andrew. "If this does get put up somewhere . . ."

"Can we be in it?" said Annie.

"Yeah, can we?" echoed Luke.

"Of course," I said.

Five months later I got an e-mail from an address I didn't recognize.

"Congratulations, your play was accepted into our festival!"

I got out my phone and texted Luke. "Would you still like to be in *Thank You Ten*?"

"Yes!" he wrote back.

Annie confirmed, our friend Andrew Neisler agreed to direct, and for the next few weeks I sat giggling as two of my closest friends simulated sex in a rehearsal room. If Luke had known the director would make him wear a thong dance belt onstage, I wonder if he would have said yes. I like to think I made up for it by introducing him to his girlfriend three years later.

"*Thank You Ten* is going to be in a festival," I told my therapist. "And I just got word that some friends want me to do it at a night of one-acts, too."

"Your first produced play!" she said. "I'd like to think I had something to do with that."

"Yeah," I said. "Well, you, Allison, and Gavin from South Africa." My own personal muse.

writing robin

It was my first day back in New York after a few weeks in San Francisco doing shows, going on ice cream crawls, and spending time with my friends and my sister. Jet lag had gotten to me, the world didn't seem real yet. My friends Jenny and Max were with me at Max's family's music store, and we were joking around when Jenny's phone rang.

"It's my mom," Jenny said. She picked up and listened for a few seconds. Her eyes, which are always wide, got even wider.

"What?" I said. "What is it?"

"Robin Williams died."

Everything around me stopped. I put my hand over my mouth and took a deep breath.

"I need to call my brother," I announced. Not only does Danny have a way of calming me down in any circumstance, he also has a preternatural ability to know about every breaking news story before anyone else. He picked up immediately.

"Danny, did you hear? Is it true?"

"Unfortunately, it is," he said.

I swallowed. "But how did it happen?" Heart attack, probably, I thought. My father had dealt with heart trouble, and he was about my father's age and build.

"They're saying it was suicide," he said, and the world went away. Through the haze I could feel Max wrapping his arms around me, and Jenny asking if I wanted to go home.

"Yes," I said.

She took me home in a cab. I sat on my couch, staring straight ahead. My phone buzzed with all kinds of messages, but the only one I remember came from Lisa Jakub.

"Hey, sis. Today is an awful day, isn't it? I love you and am here to talk if you need me."

The day passed, somehow. What I most remember is Jenny opening up a mini box of Smarties I'd brought back from a trip to Canada. The box was covered with cartoon animals smiling, and in French, German, and English, they were saying, "It will be okay!"

I folded it up and put it in my wallet. I don't believe in signs, but I wanted to then.

For the next few days I tried to ignore all the pictures of him, the Pagliacci allusions, the "Genie, you're free" memes, the many magazine articles. I would turn around tabloids with his face on them at the gym and the pharmacy. Fox News e-mailed asking if I wanted to go on Greta Van Susteren to talk about him. I did not.

I was alone with my guilt. I had just been there, in San Francisco, days before he died. If only I'd contacted him, made a plan to see him. Just months earlier I'd said that I had no desire to be in a *Mrs. Doubtfire* sequel Twentieth Century Fox had been planning. If I was to be in the spotlight, I wanted it to be because of my own goals and desires, not out of obligation. But I had been so adamant, saying that there was no way it would be good and that I wanted nothing to do with it. Had that depressed him further? I was sinking into the worst kind of magical thinking. He hadn't seen me in years. Why would it have changed anything if I'd gone to see him, or if I'd agreed to be in the sequel? Why would anything I could have said mattered?

There was a heavy, empty feeling in my chest. It felt familiar. Grief. The last time I had felt it this strongly, I was a little girl. The only way I knew how to deal with it then was creating. It was why, after my mother's funeral, I picked lemons from the backyard and offered people fresh lemonade I had made at the reception. It was why, when I was nine, I tried to write a screenplay about two teenagers solving mysteries—and had the big bad villain kill off one of their mothers. There's a reason actors are told to "use it" when they're upset. You don't go on with the show in spite of your heartbreak or grief. You go on *because* you're grieving. It's how you deal.

There was only one way I was going to cope with all my feelings about Robin's death, and that was to write. A week after his death, I put up a new post on my blog:

remembering robin

He always reminded me a little of my father.

Robin Williams, as I knew him, was warm, gentle, expressive, nurturing, and brilliant. While it can be hard for me to remember filming *Doubtfire*, I've been flooded with memories in the past few days. It's humbling to know I am one of the few people who was there for these moments, that he's no longer around to share them.

He was a creator as much as a performer. After one of my friends posted Robin's "impression of a hot dog" on Facebook, I realized she had no idea that wasn't in the script. It was supposed to be a monologue where he listed every voice he could do, but he decided to take the ones he'd been given, add more of his own, and just riff for a while. Chris Columbus, our director, would let Robin perform one or two takes with what was written, then do as many more takes as Robin had variations. Sometimes I wonder why they didn't give him at least partial screenwriting credit.

He was so quick and prolific, coming up with so many lines and bits even though there was no way we could use them all. At the end of the first dinner scene, where I said my most infamous line, he uses chopsticks like antennae to make me smile. That was a reference to a take that didn't end up in the film, where Robin was supposed to make a speech about his new job boxing and shipping cans, then turn it into a song. He went off book, as always, and before we knew what he was doing, the chopsticks were by his ears and he was freestyle rapping from the point of view of an ant railing against the humans who kept stepping on its friends.

Robin would do anything to make me and the other kids laugh. Those hand puppets that dance alongside the genie in *Aladdin*'s "Friend Like Me"? That must have been his suggestion, because Robin made those in real life. He'd break them out between takes to entertain us. "I don't like you," his left hand would say to his right. "You smell like poop!" I would laugh uproariously—I was five, so poop jokes were the height of hilarity—as his right hand

One of my first ever film scenes, but I never felt nervous. We already felt like family.

yelled back, "Well, there's no toilet paper at my house!" When he saw me watching him work on his laptop during downtime, he played a sound file of Dorothy from the *Wizard of Oz* screeching "You wicked old witch!" When we were filming the petting zoo birthday scene, he fed a pony oats out of his hat, then held it out to me and said, "Wanna wear it?" When we were filming the climactic dinner party scene, he would make his carpet bag bark like a dog under the table, then order it to be quiet. He seemed to know instinctively what we would find funny, and never had to resort to saying anything that was inappropriate for children. He was, after all, a father himself.

Robin was so on so much of the time that I was surprised to hear my mother describe him as "shy."

"When he talks to you," she told her friends, "he'll be looking down at his shoes the whole time." I figured he must have been different with grown-ups. I wouldn't see that side of him myself until a few years later, when I was invited to be part of a table read of *What Dreams May Come*. He came alive in the reading, but my strongest impression came when we saw each other for the first time that day. Robin crossed to me from across the room, crouched down to my level, and whispered, "Hi, how are you?" He asked how my family was doing, how school was, never raising his voice and only sometimes making eye contact. He seemed so vulnerable. *So this is what Mom meant,* I thought. It was as if I was seeing him for the first time. He was a *person* now.

As of this past Monday, Robin and I had not spoken in a few years. We weren't on bad terms, we had just lost track of each other. He was working in films still, I was not anymore, he still lived in California, I'd moved probably nine times since I last had his contact information. The last time I saw him, I was a freshman at NYU and he was filming *August Rush* in Washington Square Park. I went up to him while he was walking away from the set to his trailer, and called his name. He turned around, not sure what to make of the girl in the glasses and NYU hoodie calling out to him like she knew him.

"It's me!" I said. "It's Mara."

"Oh, Mara!" He told me how grown up I looked and asked how I liked NYU. It was small talk, but something about the way Robin looked at me made it feel like he truly cared. This was someone for whom everything mattered.

I wish we had talked more. I wish I had reached out more. Being a Worst Case Scenario kind of person, I've worried so many times about losing so many people I care about, but I never imagined losing Robin.

My grieving has been private. I kept off my public Facebook page and my Twitter and tried to avoid any entertainment media. Doing interviews is usually fun and easy for me, but I didn't feel I could do any then. If I was crying seeing Robin's face on the *Daily News*, I would not have been able to keep it together on cable news, and people didn't need to see that. Lisa Jakub, my big sister in *Doubtfire* and my honorary big sister in real life, wrote a beautiful blog post about her experiences with him and was able to appear on TV. She said all the things I couldn't. It reminded me of how she handled the *Doubtfire 2* announcement a few months back with such grace, while I ended up coming off a lot more brusque and dismissive than I had wanted. Life imitating art, I joked with her: in *Doubtfire*, she was the more mature older sister, while I was the little one who always blurted out the wrong thing. One of us cautious and pensive, one of us quick and outspoken. Much like the two sides of Robin, as my brother Danny pointed out: "You guys *were* him." (Matt Lawrence, who played our brother, got his physicality and charm.)

I had thought maybe the next time I saw Robin I would explain myself to him, let him know that I had loved working with him but didn't feel like we could do it as well a second time, and that being in major studio films again would mean a level of scrutiny I didn't think I could deal with. I wanted to apologize and know he understood. It hurts to know I can't.

I'm glad people are starting to talk seriously about mental health, depression, and suicide. I've discussed my OCD, anxiety, and depression in the past and will continue to do so more in the future. Mental health needs to be taken as seriously as physical health; the two go hand in hand. But I am afraid people will romanticize what Robin went through. Please don't romanticize mental anguish. I know many people who think to be an artist means you have to suffer. It's not only an incorrect assumption—there are comedians who had happy upbringings, I swear—but encouraging suffering will only hurt them and the people who care about them. Artists who struggle with mental illness, trauma, disease, addiction (often the latter is a way of self-medicating to ameliorate or cope with the first three) do not want or welcome it. I don't know if I'd consider myself an artist, but speaking as someone who sometimes makes stuff, I can say that my best work is created when I'm content and contemplative, looking back on painful times rather than in the middle of them. To focus on someone's pain instead of their accomplishments is an insult to them. As my friend Patrick put it, a person is a person first and a story second.

In the past few days I have said "thanks" and "I love you" to so many people. I'm fortunate to know people who care and have been so good to me, and it's heartening to know there are so many people who will miss Robin, too. When I got on Facebook that night, I was immediately overwhelmed and touched by how many people had kind words to say about him. Many of my friends are comedians who were inspired by him, but others have just loved his movies and comedy and had since their childhoods. If you can affect someone when they're young, you are in their heart forever. It is remarkable how many lives Robin touched, and how many people said, just as I had, that he reminded them of their fathers. I suppose—could I really end this any other way?—we're all his goddamn kids, too.

I always looked up to Robin. It seemed like everyone around me did, too. On the set of *Doubtfire*, a fourteen-year-old Danny had, after weeks of being too nervous, asked Robin, "What is it that makes you hold your audience so well? How do you do it?" Robin smiled and responded, "It's very simple, really. It's what you leave in, and what you put out."

Not leave out and put in, but leave *in* and put *out*. Danny and I are still puzzling over what he might have meant. Perhaps that it all came down to the content one left in and the energy one put out while performing. Perhaps that what one kept to oneself was as important as what was said, and it needed to be not just *left* out casually, but *put* out carefully, with thought and precision. When Danny thought it meant one thing, I thought it might mean another, and neither of us could stop thinking about it. Maybe we both wanted one last thing from Robin, guidance given to us personally, but we couldn't ever fully understand it. Maybe there really was no way he could explain how he did what he did. It was harder than it looked, but it came easily to him. All he needed was something to riff on.

One of my strongest memories of Robin didn't happen on *Doubtfire* at all, but at the table read for *What Dreams May Come* that I mentioned in my post. It was an exceptionally long script, so we stopped for lunch in the middle. Robin was in his quiet, serious mode. I wanted to make him smile, and I thought of the way he came alive when he was doing an impersonation, or when he had a character to play. I wanted to see him perform.

"Robin," I said, "I have to tell you about this guy we saw when we were filming *A Simple Wish*." We had been on location in Oklahoma, driving to the set down a dirt road, when a man in a cowboy hat flagged us down.

"Mornin'! How are you?" he drawled.

"We're fine, thanks," said the driver. "How are you?"

"I'm as fine as a hair on a frog split two ways!" he said, and let us pass. He had nothing to do with the film; he just wanted to stop us to say hello. We drove away and burst out laughing.

"He was like a character from *Oklahoma!*" I said. Robin's eyes lit up.

"'Fine as a hair on a frog!'" he kept repeating, and then he launched into a full impression of the strange, lone cowboy. Everyone laughed, and for the rest of lunch we just watched him perform. That's how I'll always remember him. The performer, performing.

WGAS live from brooklyn

MY MOTHER WAS the storyteller in the family. She knew just what to emphasize and what to gloss over, and when to get inappropriate—I always knew she had gone into some of her more blue material when she clapped her hands over my ears.

My father is different, quieter, a private and practical man. He never commanded others' attention like our mother did. "I'm a behind-the-scenes guy," he always said. But he had stories, too. At a rare quiet moment at dinner, or whenever we had guests, one of my brothers would turn to him and ask about one of his old pranks.

"Dad, did you really take the fortunes out of all the fortune cookies at a party and put in ones that said 'You will never amount to anything'?"

My father's smile was always half proud, half sheepish.

"I did, yeah."

Most of his best stories were from the time he hosted a radio show. "I learned a lot there," he said. "One of my bosses used to tell me, 'Mike, no matter what radio station you're on, it's always WGAS—Who Gives A Shit?'" It was imperative to know his audience, and remember what would interest them and what wouldn't.

It was a lesson I kept coming back to, especially in college. My program at NYU, Playwrights Horizons Theater School, was a great place to learn how to collaborate, but making some really self-serving art was practically a rite of passage. This was a school, after all, that had made it a tradition for classes of freshmen to get together and draw one another nude. A lot of my friends wanted to provoke or scare their audiences, but I just wanted to entertain. I wanted to make sure they Gave A Shit. I got the best response when I wrote about my life. People wanted to hear me talk: they no longer told me, "You ramble too much, Mara"; they said, "You've had a really interesting life, Mara."

It was what I had wanted to do since I could talk: be a storyteller, an Ashkenazi Scheherazade. For years, I had been telling myself I didn't want to be in the spotlight, but I was starting to realize I did. Maybe I would write, maybe I would act, but what I wanted more than anything was to find a way to stand onstage and tell funny stories.

"*You* want to do comedy?" My college boyfriend Sam was incredulous. At some point early in our relationship, it had been established that I was the flighty, funny one, and he was the sensible one, so it was his duty to curb my grandiosity. We were a living screwball comedy.

"Why not?" I said, a little insulted. "I think I could. You think I'm funny." One of the first times I'd gotten Sam's attention was when our Writing the Essay teacher had asked us to "make the sentence 'The woman walked down the street' interesting," and instead of bogging it down in purple prose, like many of my class-mates, I had written, "The woman walked down the street naked."

"You *are* funny," he said. "But do you know how much rejection is involved?"

"I used to be an actor," I reminded him. "I know about rejection."

"Comedians get it so much worse, though. Especially women. I don't know, honey."

Sam and I almost never fought. We were two liberal Jews minoring in social sciences; we talked things out. I should never have been surprised when he announced he was going to law school: every would-be fight seemed to end with him saying, "I don't know, honey," and explaining so precisely that I couldn't help but agree with him.

"I don't know, honey," he had said once, when I told him that in the event of a zombie uprising, I would be out on the streets kicking zombie ass. "You'd probably be hiding out in your apartment with canned food like the rest of us."

That actually offended me. "You don't think I'm brave enough?"

"Don't take it the wrong way," he said. "I'd be hiding out, too. It's safer that way."

"I don't want to do what's *safe*," I said. "I want to do what's *right*. And what's awesome."

"But you're so anxious, sweetie."

"I'm good in a crisis," I said. I was starting to feel real anger. Was this how he saw me? Anxious, helpless, effectively useless against the living dead?

Sam gave me a sidewise glance, and I knew he wanted to ask if we were really fighting about this. The last time we'd had a real fight, he'd asked me, "Mara, are you really mad at me, or are you mad at your father?"

"Just forget it," he said.

We broke up a few months later. The Night-of-the-Living-Dead fight had been a turning point in our relationship, a signifier that we didn't believe in each other the way we should have. Why had he doubted me? And why had I decided I was not going to swallow my pride that time? He had touched a nerve. Sam had known what I most wanted, my most abstract ambition, beyond being a comedian or a zombie warrior: I wanted to be a badass. Sam had denied what I most wanted.

Badasses are rampant in fiction, but they're not as rare in real life as one might believe. They know how to do everything, or at least are confident and knowledgeable enough to give people that impression. They don't worry about having to please everybody, because they make the right people happy without trying, and don't care about the rest. They are loved and feared. They exude confidence and bleed bon mots. They learn from their mistakes and take their shortcomings in stride. Even if they're short, they stand tall. Even if they aren't beautiful, they are sexy in their own way. It's impossible to surprise or shock them: they are ready for anything.

From my teenage years well into my twenties, I fantasized about being a badass more than anything else. They were never particularly elaborate fantasies: I would say the right thing at the right moment, jaws would drop, and I would walk away, perfectly curled hair blowing in the wind, perfect dark red lips curving into a smirk as I either put on or took off my sunglasses. (Being a child of the late eighties and early nineties, no one will ever be able to convince me that sunglasses aren't cool, or that dark lipstick and big curls à la Julia Roberts in *Pretty Woman* aren't the height of sexiness.) The fact that I never had to do much in these fantasies was probably telling. Deep down I think I knew that if I wanted to be a badass, I had to be good at something first.

And apparently at twenty-two I thought wearing a fedora was badass.

I figured I could be good at storytelling if I practiced. Sam might not have known it, but there was a burgeoning storytelling scene in New York City: not stand-up, exactly, though many of the stories were funny. Just real people telling real stories with a mic in front of a live audience. There was *The Moth*, a show where celebrities as well as everyday people shared their most interesting true stories; nonprofit organizations like StoryCorps that collected oral histories and anecdotes; shows like *Bare!*, *Stripped Stories*, and *Risk!* that were all about sharing one's most intimate, personal stories. These people did what I wanted to do.

Three years after I graduated from college, I told a story at a show called *The Jukebox Show* live at Union Hall in Brooklyn, and was asked to tell a story for *Risk!*. The other performers at each show asked me if I would do their shows, in turn, and I did. I felt as if I got better every time. Some shows paid, most did not. Some didn't even give drink tickets, but at that time I was inexperienced, and willing to buy into the most quixotic phrase since "happily ever after": I was doing it "for exposure." This was my scene.

The first time someone asked me to do a comedy show, I said yes. For exposure, of course. "But you know I'm a storyteller, right?"

"Yeah, but you're funny. A lot of the best comics do story-based stuff anyway. You know Chris Gethard? From *The Chris Gethard Show*? He's gonna be there, and most of his sets are stories."

The show went reasonably well. People laughed and clapped, though some of the audience didn't seem to know how to respond. Stand-up—at least, *good* stand-up—provides instant gratification, and they weren't getting that. There were murmurs of appreciation but also confusion, as if they were asking one another, "Is it okay to laugh at that?" They seemed relieved when Chris Gethard took the stage and immediately started making jokes.

Even when a comedy show went well, there was a line between the comedians and me. I felt like a human on *The Muppet Show*: a guest in their world. They weren't mean; in fact, they were often a little too nice. I knew why I was there. It was the same reason a friend asked me in passing if I would play a bit part in her Web series, then gave me top billing: I was a name. Not much

Me in my natural habitat.

of a name, a has-been, but still enough to help get attention, or at least provoke curiosity. At another time it might have felt insulting, the struggling performer equivalent of "At least you're pretty." Could I really complain, though, if it was getting me an opportunity to do what I wanted? It made me feel guilty, but so did everything. I'd already sold out. I'd sold out in advance. I wanted to be liked, and I wanted to be booked, so I never felt like I could say no.

It was March 2013, about a year after I first started telling stories, when I got an e-mail asking if I would be interested in doing a "secret comedy show in Brooklyn." I replied instantly, saying I was interested, but I'd have to look through my schedule.

The only other event on my calendar for that night was a burlesque show. It was the doing of my best friend from college. When I had first met her, she was an acting major with a very Jewish name and a very dirty mind. She had strong opinions on feminism, perfect comic timing, and a love for anything Japanese. In the years since NYU, she had reinvented herself as a burlesque performer. Now she was Iris Explosion, hilarious, smart, sexy, and powerful.

The first time I saw her perform, I had no idea what to expect. But I loved it. There was so much freedom in burlesque: beautiful women and cute boys with all kinds of bodies could do whatever they wanted onstage, as long as they ended up in some state of undress. It was DIY theater, simple and silly, but full of spectacle—in some ways, what I had loved about show choir, but with less clothing. Iris would introduce me to her friends, performers with names like Daisy Chains and Dorothy Snarker. I would never learn their "Muggle names." They were all so warm and their shows were so funny and nonjudgmental. I knew I'd be coming back.

It was an eleven o'clock showing; maybe I could go after I did the comedy show. After all, what were weekends for if not show-hopping? My roommates had long since stopped asking where I was going. It was safe to assume that every time I left the apartment after nine on the weekend, it was for Jaclyn's play or Anna's stand-up set or Nicole's concert or someone else's something or other.

I wrote back to the secret comedy show's producer. "Yes, double-checked, I'm free that night."

"Great!" he sent back. "It's at St. Vitus in Greenpoint."

Oh shit, I thought. *Greenpoint.*

Greenpoint, like Williamsburg before it, and like Bushwick after it, had rapidly become a hipster enclave. And if there's one thing that could unite New Yorkers in 2013, it was their hatred of hipsters, who had taken over large swaths of Brooklyn and parts of Manhattan, and were even starting to encroach on my beloved, sleepy borough of Queens. Unfortunately, no one could define "hipster," except by example. I'd heard it used to mean snob, would-be, trust-fund baby, hater, bore, effeminate, grad student, dropout, teenager, intellectual, idiot, racist, liberal, white person, and New Yorker. It was something some very misguided people were happy to call themselves at one time, but had since become a catchall term for someone unpleasant. Like "bro," or "Fascist."

The defining characteristic of a hipster—the thing everyone agreed on, and most hated about them—wasn't so much their taste, but their contempt and condescension toward those less cool than themselves. This knocked me down a few levels on the hipster meter, because while I have the inborn gift of pretension, I don't know what or who is cool. "Cool" is like "tall": something I know I've never been.

While the Greenpoint setting gave me pause, it was probably the least of the reasons I should have hesitated. Decidedly non-hipster friends had done shows there, and been fine. What was more worrisome was that I didn't know the comedian I'd be performing with at all. Every other comedy show I'd done had been hosted by either a friend or someone a friend could vouch for. This show had a host I'd never met. We didn't seem to have any friends in common, and his show was definitely a comedy show. I'd have to tell one of my funniest stories. I thought of the right one immediately. It was funny, self-deprecating, and had a nice arc. I could do this.

* * *

The day of the show I went to my job painting schools with the nonprofit Publicolor, came home to shower and change, and headed off to the venue. To say it was not a welcoming, familiar kind of place would be an understatement. St. Vitus wasn't just a hipster bar, it was a hipster *metal* bar.

"Oh yeah, St. Vitus," my friend Luke, of *Thank You Ten* fame, had said when I mentioned it a few days earlier. "I like that place."

"That's good to hear," I had said. He would later insist he had added something like "I don't know if it's really your scene, though."

I didn't understand metal back when all the boys in tenth grade were starting bands named Crimson Joy or DESECRATE, and I didn't understand it now. No one in my family—except my Aunt Kathy, who looks like a five-foot-tall Meg Ryan and has a poster for the movie *Heavy Metal* up in her garage—got the "metal gene." For all my mother's anger and passion, she cried at original Broadway cast recordings, and my dad is the only man of legal age I have seen drink Mike's Hard Lemonade. I once lost hearing in my left ear for twenty-four hours after a show at Le Poisson Rouge, but it was a They Might Be Giants show.

After eight years in New York, I had many memories of grungy bars, most of them East Village and Lower East Side dives that smelled like wet wood, spray paint, old craft beer, and bad decisions. I had seen undercover cops bust a guy at Blue and Gold on East Fourth Street after he knocked over a stool and tried to fight them, and I'd made out with a friend's friend who was fifteen years my senior after a long night at Double Down. I'd even lived on St. Marks Place, that former hippie and punk enclave. Okay, it was post-Giuliani, but still, I was not a babe in the woods. Something about this place, though, seemed specifically designed to make me uncomfortable. The screeching music? The way the bartenders glared when someone ordered something? The way it seemed a little too clean to be a real dive?

The bar was packed with people, none of whom I knew. Usually at least one friend would show up to support me, but here I was alone. I scanned the crowd again. They all seemed to have the same look in their eye: cynical, unimpressed. The only one who looked like she didn't belong was the smiling girl giving out tickets.

"Mara?" she called to me, and I stepped forward to the only unoccupied corner of the room, by her podium. "Hey, I'm Casey. It's so nice to meet you!"

She explained how the show would work: the host would go up first, followed by a different comedian, then I would go on.

"You'll be bringing things down a little bit with the storytelling," she said, "then we'll bring on a special guest."

"Am I the only storyteller?" I said.

She nodded, and my stomach tightened.

A young man with a mustache squeezed through the crowd. "Hey, Mara! I'm Jeff, the producer, the one who was e-mailing you. So good to have you. Do you want anything to drink?"

I must have already known I was out of my element, because I blurted out, "Do you have Prosecco?"

They just laughed, said they'd bring me a cup of wine, and pointed me down a set of rickety stairs that led to the basement "greenroom." Water dripped from a pipe in the ceiling, and there were no chairs, only a table, a podium, and fridges. No one else was there, none of the other performers, only a bartender wearing a bandana—an homage to David Foster Wallace or to Axl Rose? I wondered—who was walking up and down the stairs carrying terrible beers. On his second trip up, he slipped and fell, sending an armful of Pabst Blue Ribbon onto the basement floor.

"Are you all right?"

He didn't answer, just lay facedown where he'd fallen, shaking his head. I watched as he slowly picked himself up and got out of the way as a tall, ginger-haired man came down the stairs. In a slight Southern drawl, he told me he was the host of the show.

"Our intern Casey suggested you. She's a really big fan of the stuff you did as a kid."

"Oh, thanks, that's nice," I said.

"Yeah," he said. "Personally, I don't get it."

"Huh. Well . . ." I tried not to feel insulted. Sure, I wanted to be known more for my writing and storytelling than for what I'd done as a five-year-old, but this was just rude.

"I mean, it *is* a little weird," I said, recovering. "I don't spend all my time wondering, like, 'What happened to Larisa Oleynik from *Alex Mack*?' Or . . ." He was ten years older than me. "Or to Soleil Moon Frye, or whoever."

"Exactly," he said. "So how do you want me to introduce you?"

"Um, you can say Mara Wilson is a writer and storyteller who performs all around the city. . . . I've done *Risk!*, *Showgasm* at Ars Nova, *Funny Story*, *Tell It: Brooklyn*; I'm going to be doing *ASSSS-CAT 3000* at the Upright Citizens Brigade. . . ." He showed no recognition, just scribbled something down on his index card.

"That's good," he said, and turned away.

"Oh, um, if you want to mention my website and Twitter—"

"You can do that yourself," he said, heading up the stairs.

"Okay . . ." I paced around the basement, muttering my story to myself like a kind of rosary. I was always nervous before shows, but this felt less like nerves and more like panic.

Jeff finally came down the stairs, handing me a plastic cup of wine.

"Hey, so, Steve—who's up first, he's a comedian—he's running late, he's not here yet. So we're going to put you up first, okay?"

First? I had never gone first at a comedy show before.

Jeff was looking at me, not pushy, but expectant. He wasn't asking me to go first, he was telling me.

"Yeah, I can do that, I'll be fine," I lied.

"Great! Come up now."

We went up the stairs and into the back room. Jeff disappeared into the crowd, and I stepped up onto what seemed to be a makeshift sound booth, though no one was there. The house was full, but there still wasn't anyone I recognized. Oh, well, except for that comedian I'd seen on *Girls*, but no one I knew personally.

The host led the crowd in a chant, a kind of mock ritual, and began his bit.

"So I saw this kid in the store today, this little Puerto Rican kid . . ."

I was already getting wary. Why did it matter that he was Puerto Rican?

"And I met this kid a few years ago, when I was a substitute teacher, and I kind of ruined his life that day. . . . He came running back from the bathroom, 'cause he couldn't work his zipper and he really needed to shit. . . ."

Everyone was laughing. This guy was a teacher?

"... And you know, he's a little Puerto Rican kid, God knows what the fuck he eats. ..."

More laughter.

"... So I tried to help him with his zipper ... but I couldn't get it in time ... and then ... he shit his pants. ..."

The crowd roared, and I gulped the rest of my wine. So they liked shit jokes and laughing at children. Good to know.

I took a breath, crushed my plastic cup with one hand, and breathed out. All right, enough pretension, enough White Guilt. If I stayed too long on my high horse, I'd get vertigo. This wasn't my ideal opener, but I still had to perform.

"All right, welcome to the stage ..." The host took out his card and read, "A storyteller who tells stories all over the city ..."

"Um, excuse me," I said, stepping down off the platform and into the wall of people.

"... Mara Wilson!"

"Sorry—'scuse me—sorry—that's me. ..."

The host put the mic in the stand and stepped away. Ten seconds later I pushed past the last row of people and up onto the stage.

"So many people," I said as I adjusted the mic down a foot. "Sometimes I feel like a mouse in a world full of Lennys."

No response. Really? No one in the audience had read *Of Mice and Men*?

"Well, I've never been cool," I began.

Oh shit, I realized immediately. How could I have been so stupid? How could I have forgotten the principles of WGAS? The first thing to do is get the audience on your side, and I'd already lost them: I'd told a Greenpoint audience I wasn't cool.

"And, uh, anyway, I've always been really bad at anything athletic. The years I was supposed to be playing soccer or doing gymnastics, I was too busy sitting in front of a camera for eight hours a day. . . ."

Why didn't I cut that part? I didn't have to talk about acting. Now they knew I not only wasn't cool but was an uncool has-been.

". . . I probably should have signed up for dance or something, because PE was the sketchiest thing you could do for PE credit. The teacher's assistant was rolling joints in class and the kid who sat in front of me said he'd been in Juvenile Hall for 'messing up a Carl's Jr. real bad. . . .'"

Someone laughed. Or coughed. Two minutes down, eight more to go. Cold sweat was breaking out along my forehead. I had to keep going.

". . . I didn't do a damn thing in that class. I used to tell the teacher I couldn't run because I had TMJ."

No laughs, no murmurs, even. ". . . After I failed PE, I thought my dad had signed me up for a nighttime dance class at a local dance studio, which was bad enough, because I figured all the cool choir kids and cheerleaders who took dance there would know how awful a dancer I was. But when I got to the dance studio, all the kids had gone home, everyone there was over fifty, and Barry Manilow was playing. This was not a dance class, this was an *aerobics* class."

Please, I thought, *someone laugh, someone just react to something I'm saying.* But they didn't. No one heckles a storyteller, they just ignore her.

"So then, it's the day of the dance studio's recital—the theme is United We Dance—and I'm dressed in black stretch pants and an oversize black shirt that says 'JUMP' in gold fabric paint. I get onstage with the rest of them, and I *know* some of the coolest kids from school are performing with their hip-hop and jazz classes, so they're in the audience, too, and then the announcer says, 'Up next we have our adult aerobics dance class performing to "Jump Shout Boogie," and the fact that these ladies can do it at their age is a testament to our program!' And I squeezed my eyes shut tight and thought, *I've got to get out of here....* But I couldn't...."

Years of acting classes, and I'd never connected to a memory like this. My eyes were shut, and I was fifteen years old, reliving at once every embarrassing and terrifying experience of feeling out of place and alone. Ten again, invited to party by a nineteen-year-old I'd met on a charity cruise, who knew I was an actor in L.A. like she was. I'd been to parties before, Hollywood parties, even, including one where I'd seen Courtney Love flailing on a dance floor, but never one like Amber's, and never without a chaperone. People spilled out from stucco apartments into a courtyard, where music blared and buckets of beer splashed out into the pool. It looked like one of the parties they had on *Melrose Place*, or a beer commercial. Amber was there, showing me the Ticket to Round Two she'd gotten on *Singled Out*, and then she wasn't, and I was terrified, feeling even younger than ten, feeling like I was four and lost at Disneyland again. I used someone's wall phone to call home, and waited for my brother Danny to come get me, playing Nintendo 64 in a stranger's apartment while a drunk guy in his twenties asked if I wanted to go to Universal Studios with him tomorrow.

The audience was still there when I opened my eyes.

"...One of the cool kids, Fernando, tried to talk to me after, but was laughing so hard he couldn't say anything besides 'Mara...' That show was the most humiliating moment of my life...."

Until now.

"... On the way home, I thought about how I used to tell my PE teacher about how bullshit his class was, because it was unfair to different athletic abilities and should just be graded on effort. And he told me, 'Mara, we *do* grade on effort.'"

A sweat drop rolled down from my temple, and I took a deep breath.

"... So now I *do* work out and exercise regularly, because I have seen what happens when you don't. Thanks, I'm Mara," I said, completely neglecting to add my last name, let alone website or Twitter, and stepped off the stage.

"Let's hear it for Mara," the host called, to a smattering of applause, as I pushed through the crowd to the bar.

For the first time in my life, I knew I needed a drink.

I like alcohol, but I tend to forget it exists, and that I'm over twenty-one and can enjoy it whenever I please. Depriving myself of joys is one of the great joys of my subconscious. I also tend to forget I have ice cream in my freezer, and about the entire concept of masturbation.

"Just whatever white wine you have, please," I said to the bartender. He handed me a plastic cup, and I slammed it back as if it were a shot. The warmth spread through me, uncoiling the tightness in my chest and stomach. I asked too politely for another. As he handed it over, I caught something familiar out of the corner of my eye.

There, directly to my left, was Zach Galifianakis.

Oh shit. Of course, the "special guest." Zach Galifianakis, a world-famous comedian, had taken time off from promoting his two new movies to perform tonight, and had seen me die onstage.

I tried to bury myself in my phone, but someone touched my arm. It was Ben, a comedian acquaintance I'd met only once or twice before. He knew I had bombed. He didn't try to hide it.

"At least now you know what it's like to do a shitty show," he said.

"That's true," I said. "Can't get much worse than that, can it?"

"Oh no, it can," he said. "And it probably will. But at least you're familiar with it now."

The bar was starting to blur. Three drinks in, and I was numb.

It was time to go home; I didn't think I had the strength to go to Iris's burlesque show. I walked out into the street, everything blurry, and put my hand up. Cabs are my one vice, my getaway, and all I wanted was to be out of there as soon as possible. The smell of metal rose up from a grate on the sidewalk—the odor equivalent of the taste of fear in your mouth. It can be smelled all over New York.

I hadn't been afraid to move to New York, not at first. I hadn't thought about it at all.

"You know, back in the seventies I heard stories about mob shootings happening at the CBS studios in New York," my father had told me not long after I'd decided to go to NYU.

"It's not like that anymore, Dad," I said, adding, "but I'll stay away from CBS and the mob, just in case."

The day he dropped me off at college, I had gawked at the buildings from the moment we got off the train, drawing closer to him. I felt smaller with every block.

"People have been asking me if I'm nervous about you moving here," he said, once we were in my dorm room. "I told them, 'Mara's always been very independent, I know she'll do well.' And you will."

He gave me a hug, told me he loved me, and left. As soon as the door closed, I started to cry. I was alone in a new, enormous city. I didn't know how to get around. I'd never even seen the campus. I was terrified, and there was nothing I could do but get used to it.

New York, I soon learned, wasn't so much scary as it was *indifferent*. In Los Angeles, I had felt judged. In New York, I felt ignored. Sometimes that was what I wanted: to disappear. But sometimes I wanted to be cared for, to belong, and I had to find that myself, because the city would not provide it on its own. New York had once had a reputation for "chewing you up and spitting you out." It doesn't do that anymore. Now it just swallows you.

Back in Greenpoint, no cabs were coming, so I stumbled down the stairway into the subway station, gripping the handrail, my fear of slipping and falling and terminal brain injury overpowering my fear of germs. I swiped my MetroCard and paced up and down the platform, as I always do, waiting for the train. This was the notorious G train, G as in "Godot," a train that comes when it wants to or not at all. But it's the only direct route from north Brooklyn to Queens, where I live.

Queens isn't hip like Brooklyn, or wealthy and glamorous like Manhattan. It doesn't have the hip-hop history of the Bronx, and it's not a punch line like Staten Island. It doesn't try to be cool. It doesn't try to be anything.

"Queens," I tell my friends, "is where your grandmother lives." It's the middle sister borough. That's why I like it.

I put in my earbuds and tried to find good comfort music. "Midnight Radio" from *Hedwig and the Angry Inch* came on.

"All the misfits, and the losers," sang John Cameron Mitchell, "Well, you know you're rock and rollers...."

Not tonight, I wasn't.

"Fucking hipsters," I muttered. Then I felt a pang. Badasses don't care what other people think. That would never be me. I cared too much. I cared about everything.

The G train pulled up, surprisingly punctual and surprisingly empty, and I took a seat by the door, weaving my arm through the metal bars, steadying my feet on the ground. Steadying myself.

Sometimes it helped to talk to myself the way I spoke to the kids I worked with at Publicolor, or while nannying. I always said things to them I wished someone had said to me when I was younger. No one had ever told me it was okay to make a mistake.

"What did we learn?" I'd once asked when a girl named Ava knocked a glass of milk off the edge of the table and onto the floor.

"That Ava's an idiot," said her brother.

Oh well. It still worked with *me*.

It was one night, I told myself, one bad show. This was going to happen at some point, and it could have been much worse. I was doing pretty well if this was the worst experience I'd had on a stage in New York. Besides, if it were all easy, I wouldn't like it. When I had a good night, it wouldn't feel deserved.

This night, I realized, was the kind of thing I'd been afraid of when I worried about my life after college. Living without Sam, embarrassing myself in public, telling my stories to people who weren't even listening. I was living my fears. "Live your fear." Why didn't we teach kids that? Why wasn't *that* in a graduation speech? Commencement speakers should start telling the truth: "You're going to fuck up, but most of the time, that's all right."

The G came to a halt at Court Square and I clambered out, climbing up the stairs from the platform. When I got to the top, I paused, not sure where to go. I could transfer to the 7 train, which would take me home, or the M, which would take me into Manhattan. Suddenly, I didn't want to go home. I followed the signs to the M, and settled into a corner of the more crowded train.

Someone *had* told me it was okay to make a mistake, I realized. My friends, my teachers, my father—several people had. I had just never believed it.

When the train stopped at Delancey-Essex Street on the Lower East Side, I stepped off in one fluid movement and walked the five blocks north and east, holding my head a little higher. The bouncer glanced at my card and let me into the room. "Spanish Bombs" was playing, and I immediately saw a friendly face: a friend's girlfriend, who was selling tickets and smiling at me. As soon as I pushed through the curtain into the performance space I heard someone call out, "Mara!"

The Parkside Lounge's Saturday Night Burlesque Show, where everybody knows your name. It wasn't Iris, but one of her friends, half of a gay married couple we called "The Dandies." They were two talented Edwardian- and Victorian-inspired artists who seemed to function as a unit; the only time I ever saw them argue was when one messed up the tea ceremony. He rushed up to hug me.

"Teddy," I said, "I just did the worst show I've ever done."

"Well, come sit down and have a drink," he said. "Watch my husband take off his clothes."

He pulled me into a chair in the front row. Someone's hand was on my shoulder, someone else wanted to say hi. I felt a surge of affection for them all. They were pierced, tattooed, wisecracking, and welcoming. The ones who had also been in show choir, Drama Club, or the Gay Straight Alliance in high school. The ones who had also failed PE. They saw me as one of their own. I told them how awful my show had gone, and they laughed, and they listened. To one another, we were all badasses.

The show was a haze of glitter and sequins, featuring acts inspired by Dungeons & Dragons and "The Call of Cthulhu." A little too nerdy or too out there for some people, but for me, it was just right. Many of the performers were people I'd seen at storytelling shows. There is a surprising amount of overlap between the storytelling and burlesque communities, maybe because they both, in a way, involve getting naked. People who choose to be vulnerable are rare. People who manage to do it well are even more so.

Someday, I would figure it out. Storytelling, and everything else. At the very least, I had found my people. I was home.

acknowledgments

FIRST, I OWE thanks to my incredible editor at Penguin, the wise, multitalented, dynamic Lindsey Schwoeri. I can't imagine having trusted anyone else with the most intimate details of my life. Thank you for keeping me on track, working tirelessly, and understanding (among other things) the difference between "Zach" and "Zack." You are a badass.

Another badass deserving of thanks: my wonderful agent, Alyssa Reuben. Resolute, brilliant, and endlessly professional, you still manage to feel like a big sister.

To my first readers, Annie Dow, Max Ash (the Max from Goddess Oracle and Writing Robin), Max Reuben (the Max from the other essays), Alessandra Dreyer, Lukas Fauset, Patrick LaVictoire, Dave Grilli, Alex Kveton, Katharine Heller, Jenny "Zombie" Jaffe, Anne Thériault, Josh Gondelman, Allison Shrestha, Jaclyn Scoville, Arica Tuesday, Sara Arnold, and all the Wilson siblings, a special thank-you for your patient and thoughtful critiques, as well as your friendship. Extra-special thanks to all the members of the Playwrights of Playwrights, in all its forms, and the New York

City storytelling community, where a lot of these stories took shape.

I want to thank the teachers and mentors who came into my life at the right time, especially Laurie, Richard Wicklund, Steve Saracino, Kristen Gatley Vollman, Bonnie Carpenter, Laura Levine, Marleen Pennison, Tomi Tsunoda, and Jeni Mahoney.

To my many on-set care takers; to Bonnie Liedtke, my child-hood agent, and John Homa, my childhood acting coach, you were guiding lights in what is so often a cruel industry. I will always be grateful I had you.

Much gratitude to Jim Strader and Herdi Vandriec for field-ing requests and sending the "Just making sure you got this" e-mails I so sorely needed.

Thanks to everyone at Cracked, especially Mack Leighty and Dan O'Brien, for giving me a platform, and for allowing me to say, "Hey, I literally wrote the article on child stars."

I am much obliged to Joseph Fink and Jeffrey Cranor for giv-ing me a chance to be creepy, for giving me a chance to See Amer-ica Right, and for telling me "Yeah, that's normal" every time I panicked.

A very loud THANK-YOU to my CAMP britches. Celebra-tory s'mores all around!

To L.A. (not the city), thank you for the reality checks. I could not have done this without you.

Dad, I will never know how you did it all. I love you to pieces. B., mahal kita, Inay.

Last, I want to thank my *first* first readers, my first audience, and my built-in best friends, Danny, Jon, Joel, and Anna Wilson. You are my favorite people in the world, and I know a lot of people. Thank you for listening to my stories, for knowing me better than anyone ever can or will, and for giving me a nephew and a niece who have, in turn, shown me the meaning of unconditional love. I love you all more than you will ever know. See you at the rattlesnake sign.